Guiding Light

Inspired to Be Genuine
CYCLE A

Homilies by Fr. Joe Robinson

Shepherds of Christ Publications
P.O. Box 627
China, Indiana 47250 USA

Toll free USA: (888) 211-3041
Tel: (812) 273-8405
Fax: (812) 273-3182
Email: info@sofc.org
http://www.sofc.org

ISBN: 978-1-934222-40-9

First Printing: 2013
Second Printing: April 2014

Dedicated to Pope Francis

In Honor
of Our
Beloved Priests

The Mass

The Mass is the sacrifice of Calvary –
sacramentally made present.
As members of the mystical body
of Christ, we are united to all
the Masses going on around the
world this day. Our lives are an
offering to the Father, in union
with Jesus in the Holy Sacrifice
of the Mass, in the Holy Spirit,
through the intercession of
our Heavenly Mother –
with all the angels and saints
and the souls in purgatory.
We are one united to the Mass.
Tremendous grace can be
outpoured on the earth from
doing this, living in the Father's
will in love – united to the
Mass, the sacrifice of Calvary –
sacramentally made present.
God enlists our help today –

Oh the gift of the Mass –
Oh the gift of the priest –

Jesus is truly present in His Divinity
and humanity in the Eucharist –

He says:
"This is My Body,
  This is My Blood,
  given up for you."

Rita Robinson Ring, Co-founder
Shepherds of Christ Ministries

We want Adoration Chapels
around the world –
The Mighty Medicine

Table of Contents
Cycle A - 2013 / 2014

Certificate of Marriage

I, the undersigned, do hereby certify, that on the 25 day of June A.D. 19 36
in the church of St. Boniface I joined in the

Holy Bonds of Matrimony

William M. Robinson and Alice Weber

according to the rites of the Holy Roman Catholic Church.

Witness: Henry J. Robinson
Marie Weber

Rev. John H. Schwarz
Pastor

Dedicated to William and Alice Robinson.

Our Mother and Father married on
June 25, 1936 in St. Boniface Church, Cincinnati.

1st Sunday of Advent
November 28, 2010

INTRODUCTION – (Isaiah 2:1-5; Romans 13:11-14; Matthew 24:37-44) The prophet we hear in today's first reading lived over 700 years before Christ. Most probably he had witnessed the destruction of the northern kingdom of Israel by the Assyrians, fierce warriors who came from what is modern day Iraq. The southern kingdom of Israel, centered in Jerusalem, lived in fear and trembling that the same fate awaited them. In spite of great turmoil, his message is a message of peace, a peace we continue to yearn for. It is a peace, however, that flows only from walking in God's ways.

HOMILY – A lady, raised as a vegetarian, hardly ever saw a piece of meat growing up. When she married a man who loved meat, they had meat all the time. One Thanksgiving while they and their children were having dinner, the husband announced to the children: "Your mother didn't know what a turkey was until she met me." (*Readers Digest*, Dec. 2010/Jan. 2011, pg 151) I hope everyone had a nice Thanksgiving.

Today we begin a new Church year with the first Sunday of Advent. I want to tell you about a Scotsman who was calling his dentist to ask about the price of a tooth extraction. Scotsmen are famous for being exceedingly thrifty. The dentist told him it would cost $85. "$85!!! Huv ye no'got anythin' cheaper?" "That's the normal charge," said the dentist. "Whit aboot if ye didnae use any anesthetic?" "That's unusual, sir, but I could do it and knock $15 off." "Whit aboot if ye used one of your dentist trainees and still without an anesthetic?" "I can't guarantee their professionalism and it'll be painful. But the price could drop to $40." "How aboot if ye make it a trainin' session, ave yer student do the extraction with the other students watchin' an learnin'?" "It'll be good for the students," mulled the dentist, "and it's going to be very traumatic, but I'll charge you $5." "Ah, now yer talkin' laddie! It's a deal," said the Scotsman. "Can ye confirm an appointment for the wife next Tuesday?" (from an email)

It's normal for people to want to know how much something costs, even how much it will cost us to get into heaven or how much we need to pray for someone who has died to help them get into heaven. That was one of the questions that kept coming up in high school religion class: how far can we go and still stay in the state of grace; how late can we be for Mass or how early can we leave after Communion and still fulfill our obligation. For some of us older folks, if we ate a little meat on Friday, how much is too much. We tend to ask what's the least amount it will cost us – the least amount of sacrifice we have to make to be able to get to heaven; to go "rejoicing to the house of the Lord."

Another manifestation of this kind of thinking is when we wonder when do we need to be ready to meet the Lord. If we're living a life without God, we try to calculate how long we might have before we could die and not be reconciled with God. Some people might be guilty of the sin of presumption, thinking there will be no consequences for ignoring God's law because God is all good so we don't have to worry about being ready. As we all get ready to celebrate the birth of our Savior, today's scriptures tell us we need to do more. We need to get ready for the day he will come again, not as a baby but as our glorified, risen Lord. Paul says, that day is closer than when we first believed. Jesus tells us that day will catch us off guard if we're not ready; it will hit us like a flood, like a thief when we're asleep, in the middle of the day while we're at work or fixing dinner.

Advent means "coming" and although we are touched by the humble coming of our God as an infant to save us, it's also the coming of an adult Christ that we must be thinking of. Will he be a stranger to us and will we be a stranger to him? There's one sure way we will not meet as strangers, and that is to pray. We'll never have a relationship with God (or for that matter with anyone else) unless we put time aside to nurture that relationship. If we want to know what is the minimum amount of time we can get by with, it's not going to amount to much of a relationship. The second thing it will cost us if we want to go rejoicing to the house of the Lord is to "conduct ourselves properly;" i.e., as he has taught us. Paul gives us a few examples of improper behavior which he describes as making "provision for the desires of the flesh." Obviously Paul is talking about the desires and cravings of the flesh that are forbidden. A third thing it will cost us to stay on the good side of our creator is to do good works, to love our neighbor as ourselves.

As I conclude, I want to leave you with one thought for this week: come to one of our holy hours this week on Wednesday morning or Friday afternoon. Both of them will be dedicated to prayer for the unborn as our Holy Father and bishops have requested we do. One of the ways we can change the world is through prayer. It is only appropriate that as we prepare to celebrate the birth of a child who came to save us, we pray for those many others who are soon to be born that they be loved and cherished and not be robbed of life and be thrown into a recycle bin.

If you have some other priority to help you be ready to meet the Lord, then that's what needs attention. Paul tells us if we want to go rejoicing to the house of the Lord, it is now the hour to wake from sleep. Amen.

Second Sunday of Advent
December 5, 2010

INTRODUCTION – (Isaiah 11:1-10; Romans 15:4-9; Matthew 3:1-12) The first reading for all our Sunday readings throughout Advent this year as well as our first reading for all Christmas Masses comes from the Book of the Prophet Isaiah. The historical setting for today's first reading goes back 700 years before Christ. It was a time of great distress for Israel. The Assyrians had literally annihilated all of the area north of Jerusalem, an area known as the northern kingdom. It was very likely Jerusalem would be the next victim of the Assyrian army. In spite of all this, we hear in today's reading a message of hope – a promise of great blessings to those who have remained faithful to God. A great leader, filled with the Spirit of God, would usher in these blessings. This leader would come from the royal house of David – that is what Isaiah meant when he identifies this leader as a shoot that would sprout from the stump of Jesse. "Stump" is equivalent to "roots" here. Jesse was the father of King David, as I'm sure you all know.

HOMILY – A teacher asked her Sunday school class: "If I sold my house and my car, and everything I owned, and gave all the money to the poor, would I get into heaven?" The children all answered, "No!" Then she asked, "If I cleaned the church every day, mowed the yard, and kept everything neat and tidy, would I get into heaven?" Again the answer was, "No!" "Well, then," she asked, "what do I need to do to get into heaven?" One of her five-year-old students answered, "You gotta be dead!" (from *Laughter, the Best Medicine, Reader's Digest*, pg 308) (As I hope we all know, the child was correct, but there's a bit more to it than that!)

In Isaiah's time, 700 years before Christ, God's people believed there would be some kind of existence after death in a place called Sheol. In their conception of Sheol, there was nothing but darkness, worms, dust and the only food was clay. It was a place of utter inactivity. There is no work, no thought, no knowledge, no wisdom, no praise of God, and God does not remember those in Sheol. There is neither pain nor joy – it is as empty of life as it can be. This concept was probably inherited from Mesopotamian mythology and is fairly descriptive of what the grave would be like. Apparently the Assyrians and Babylonians didn't have quite as vivid an imagination as the Egyptians when it came to the afterlife. As regards God's people, we have to understand God didn't reveal everything at once. For many centuries before Jesus, the Jews thought of the afterlife as I have described it. Because they believed that God was just and fair, they logically concluded that the reward for a good life, as well as the punishment for an evil life, came to a person in this life, not in the next. Of course, we know it doesn't always work that way. Good people do suffer and evil people sometimes literally get by with murder. That's the problem the whole book of Job is wrestling with – why do good people suffer?

700 years before Christ, Isaiah described in beautiful poetry a world of peace and justice, and he describes it the only way he knew how to describe it. It will be ruled by a king, a shoot from the stump of Jesse, endowed with the gifts of the Spirit of God. Perhaps you noticed in today's first reading the mention of the seven gifts of the Holy Spirit that we learned about in catechism: wisdom, understanding, counsel, fortitude (i.e. strength), knowledge, piety and fear of the Lord. I don't know if we will ever see a world like Isaiah describes. Isaiah's poetic description would require a complete transformation of

nature. In light of further revelation given to us since Isaiah's time, and especially in light of what Jesus has revealed to us, it is easy to envision heaven as Isaiah describes it in today's reading. In this sense, Isaiah's message continues to be a message of hope. No matter how bad things may become, God has plans of great happiness for those who faithfully follow the leadership of this ideal king from the root of Jesse.

Advent is a time of hope, but it is also a time of preparation for the blessings for which we hope. This is where John the Baptist comes in. His job was to prepare people for the coming of God's kingdom. If we want to prepare ourselves, we have to listen to John. We can't just take it for granted that getting to heaven is an entitlement any more than the Jews could presume they had it made because they were Jews. John told them, "do not presume to say to yourselves, 'We have Abraham for our father.'" John said God is looking for good fruits. Several times in Scripture, Jesus clarified what is meant by "good fruits." We can summarize what good fruits means by saying it means loving God above all things and loving our neighbor as ourselves, but there's a lot that's meant by "love."

John the Baptist is no longer with us (Herod Antipas saw to that). The Church now takes up the cry of John during the season of Advent and calls us to "prepare the way of the Lord ..." There are lots of preparations that go on during this time of the year, preparations for gatherings with friends and family, preparations for gift giving, preparations for parties, etc. Let's not forget the most important preparation of all, to prepare our heart to receive our Lord and Savior with greater faith and devotion than ever this Christmas. Amen.

Feast of the Immaculate Conception
December 8, 2007

INTRODUCTION – (Genesis 3:9-15, 20, Ephesians 1:3-6, 11-12, Luke 1:26-38) The feast today is about Mary's conception, that from the instant she began to exist on this earth, indeed from her very conception, she was holy, without sin and filled with God's grace. The gospel today can confuse us somewhat because it tells us about Jesus' conception. It was read, however, because of the greeting the angel used in appearing to her: "Hail, full of grace." Our feast celebrates that there was no moment in Mary's life when there was sin, no moment when God's grace did not fill her.

HOMILY – As we listen in on this conversation between Mary and the Angel, we learn both about Mary and about the child she will give birth to. Mary's child would be Son of the Most High and king forever. He will be called "holy, the Son of God."

This is why Mary was "full of grace," so she could give birth to God's own Son, who would be the source of all holiness. We need to know this, not so that we can put Jesus and Mary on a pedestal and admire them from afar. Jesus, the holy one of God came to us so that we too can become holy. This is what St. Paul tells us in today's second reading: "God chose us in him to be holy and blameless in his sight."

Most of us do not think of our vocation as a call to holiness. We all want to get to heaven, but most of us think of holiness as reserved for other people, like St. Francis or Mother Teresa. Most of us are content to leave holiness for someone else. We just want to get through heaven's doors. But no one will get to heaven unless they are holy, for holiness means being close to God and sharing God's life. And that's what God's grace does for us: it unites us with God and allows us to share in God's life. If we are in God's grace, then, we are holy people.

Two stories we heard today tell us of our vocation to be holy: The story in our first reading is about Adam and Eve, our first parents, who originally were very close to God and in their union with God, they were very happy. That was the symbol of the Garden of Eden. But they got greedy! They wanted to be equal to God. The evil one knew how to manipulate them and lead them to ignore God's command. As a result they lost all they had. The second story in the gospel illustrates Mary's constant attitude of being willing to say "yes" to God, an openness that prepared the way for the Son of God to come to us.

When we were baptized we were filled with God's life, we were born again in God's grace. The very same grace that filled Mary at the moment of her conception, filled us when we were baptized. None of us will ever be as holy as Mary was. She got a head start on all of us. But if we follow the example of Mary, always ready to say "yes" to God, that will lead us to holiness and to the joy and peace and love that comes with it.

3rd Sunday of Advent
December 12, 2010

INTRODUCTION – (Isaiah 35:1-6a, 10; James 5:7-10; Matthew 11:2-11) If you or I could change our world to make it better, what would we do to change it? Today Isaiah describes to God's people (most probably those who were still in exile) what God's plans were to make things better. God would start with the land, turning their desert, arid lands into gardens bursting with vegetation and beauty, comparable to the costal areas where the land was fertile and there was adequate rainfall, such as Lebanon, Carmel (which is today Haifa) and Sharon. Transforming the land was just a beginning. Those who were weak, sick, blind and lame would be freed of their affliction. It would be a return to the Garden of Eden where God's people would be crowned with everlasting joy. What a beautiful picture of salvation Isaiah presents. As Matthew tells us in today's gospel, God's work of creating a new world begins with Jesus. St. James tells us in the second reading that as we hope for a new world, we must be patient and steadfast in our faith.

HOMILY – A lady who was working as a phone-order representative for a textbook publisher tells this story. One very busy day many customers had been put on hold. When she took one of her waiting calls, she heard an annoyed lady on the line muttering to herself: "Darn, damn, damn, darn, darn!" She smiled and asked: "What may I help you with today?" After a brief silence the caller said: "I'm sorry I got carried away talking to myself here; I guess I was in too much of a hurry. I would like to place an order for some books." The lady taking the order said, "That's hardly the worst thing I heard today. Now, first I need your name." "Oh dear," the caller said, "how embarrassing. My name is Sister Patience." (from *Laughter, the Best Medicine, Reader's Digest*, pg 293).

This little story might help us remember what St. James tells us in today's second reading: "Be patient, brothers and sisters, until the coming of the Lord." In our gospel, John the Baptist is now in prison. Was he becoming impatient because our Lord hadn't rescued him? Didn't Jesus claim, quoting Isaiah, that he had been sent "to proclaim liberty to captives?" (Lk 4:18) One gets the impression from John's preaching that he expected the Kingdom of God to come in a very short time. On the other hand, there's always the possibility he was sending his disciples to Jesus so they would learn about Jesus and the marvelous things he was doing. I'm sure no one could know the motivation John the Baptist had for sending his disciples to Jesus to ask whether he was the one who is to come. Prophets can see things much more clearly than the rest of us can. The main point St. Matthew is making for his readers is that the work of Jesus shows that God's kingdom has begun. The answer of Jesus to John's disciples as to whether he is the expected Messiah sounds as if it comes right out of our first reading from Isaiah: "the blind see, the lame walk, the deaf hear, etc."

How often have we asked this same question of Jesus as John did: "Are you he who is to come; are you the one who is supposed to save the world? Then, why aren't you doing it? Look at what a mess the world is in, or look at how I am suffering, or how a friend is suffering. Why did that young person have to die so young?" A lot of people have offered an answer as to why there is suffering. Answers range from the atheist who says there is no God to the person who concludes God just doesn't care, to the philosopher who says just get as much pleasure out of this life as you can and be happy with what you get. There are many answers to suffering among great thinkers. The best answer is that Jesus is the savior. Once, when people thought Jesus was talking crazy (like eat my flesh and drink my blood), and they started walking away, Jesus turned to the apostles and asked: "Are you going to leave me too?" Peter answered: "Master, to whom shall we go? You have the words of eternal life. We have come to believe and are convinced that you are the Holy One of God." After I've explored all other options to explain suffering, Jesus is the only answer that makes sense to me. It takes a lot of faith sometimes to keep trusting that God is in the process of bringing about his kingdom of love and justice and peace.

St. James tells us today, "You must be patient. Make your hearts firm, because the coming of the Lord is at hand." A firm faith gives us hope, and hope keeps us from despair; even more it is a source of joy helping us to trust in the life that is to come, a life "crowned with everlasting joy" as Isaiah says.

Fourth Sunday of Advent
December 19, 2010

INTRODUCTION – (Isaiah 7:10-14; Romans 1:1-7; Matthew 1:18-24) Conflict in the Middle East is not a new thing. Our first reading takes us back 700 years before Christ. It was as complicated a political situation as it is today. There are four kings you have to keep track of. Tiglath-pileser III was king over the Assyrians. (You won't be quizzed on that name.) The Assyrians were the dominant power in the Middle East. They were an especially cruel and powerful nation whose capital was located in what is today northern Iraq. There was a king of Jerusalem, named Ahaz, who ruled the southern part of the Holy Land, and a king in Samaria who ruled the northern part of the Holy Land. Further north was the king in Damascus. The two northern kings wanted King Ahaz in Jerusalem to join them in an alliance to go to war against the Assyrians. Ahaz refused, so the two northern kings were going to attack Jerusalem, and replace Ahaz with someone who would cooperate with them. Ahaz decided to call on Assyria for protection. This is where our first reading comes in – an extremely important passage in the Book of the Prophet Isaiah.

Isaiah warned Ahaz not to get involved with Assyria for they were too powerful. He promised, "God would keep the king and Jerusalem safe." The other two kings would soon be destroyed. Ahaz did not have enough faith in God. Isaiah tried to offer Ahaz a sign. Ahaz protested, but Isaiah offered one anyway. For Ahaz the sign would be that he would soon have a son to succeed him as king. He had no offspring at this time for he had sacrificed his only son to the Canaanite God, Moloch. Ahaz' son would be called by the symbolic name Emmanuel for he would be a sign that God was with his people. It is a good possibility that the son Ahaz eventually had was Hezekiah who turned out to be a good leader and a king who was faithful to God. St. Matthew saw in this promise of Isaiah a greater depth of meaning. He saw that Jesus fulfilled this promise perfectly by being born of a virgin and by being a sign to us that God is with us.

HOMILY – A mother tells the story of her five-year-old daughter and three-year-old son watching the Christmas story on TV. As she was preparing dinner she heard her littlest one ask his older sister, "What is a virgin?" The mother said, "As my mind raced to come up with an answer, her five-year-old daughter answered it, 'It's a lady who eats all her vegetables." (*The Joyful Noiseletter*, December, 1999)

One afternoon after hearing the Divine Praises at benediction, a family were leaving church and their little third-grade son asked his parents, "What's a most chased spouse?" The mother replied: "A chaste spouse is someone's husband or wife who is good and pure and holy. Why do you ask?" "Our prayers in church called St. Joseph Mary's most chaste spouse," he said. Mom asked, "What do you think it means?" A little embarrassed the boy answered, "Well, I thought it meant that all the girls chased after him, but Mary got him in the end." (*The*

Joyful Noiseletter, December, 1998)

St. Luke's version of the angel's annunciation to Mary is very popular. Our one stained glass window pictures the scene and there are many, many famous paintings of the event. I can't remember ever having seen one picture that depicts today's gospel from St. Matthew of the annunciation to St. Joseph. Luke's annunciation has a much greater poetic beauty, but Matthew's annunciation to Joseph has a message of its own. Matthew's account reveals some of the anxiety Joseph experienced before Jesus was born, and perhaps, as a result Mary had some anxieties as well. We will soon sing: Silent Night, Holy Night, all is calm, all is bright. Even with angels singing and kings arriving, all was not calm or bright. In the Jewish tradition, marriage was a two-step process. First there was a formal exchange of consent before witnesses. The second step was at a later time (usually about a year later) when the groom took the bride to his home. Even before they came to live together, legally they were married. The gospels do not tell us what emotions Mary may have gone through after the visit of the angel. St. Luke stresses the joy she felt in the beautiful hymn, the Magnificat. But she may have experienced some fear too, knowing now she was going to have a child but not by the man she was committed to. Would Joseph accept her? If she were to be judged as sinful according to Deuteronomy (22:20-21), the penalty would be execution by stoning. So many particulars we do not know, but we do know, especially with this story about Joseph, there must have been some anxious moments. I can't imagine that Mary would not have confided in Joseph, but we don't know what Joseph thought about the situation. Saints and theologians and scripture scholars have differed on what might have motivated Joseph to divorce her. He planned on doing it quietly which means he was not going to call for a public trial. Was he afraid that he was not worthy of the honor of being married to Mary and of being the legal father of this holy child she was bearing? Or was he afraid, being a righteous man as Matthew describes him, that he was breaking the law of God by accepting her into his home. All we know is that it must have been a troubling time. But a vision put Joseph at peace and obediently, like Mary did when the angel appeared to her, he did what the angel asked him to do. As in Luke's gospel, the angel that appeared to Joseph affirmed that Mary conceived miraculously through the Holy Spirit and her son would be God with us. This is an important theme in Matthew that in Jesus God is with us. It opens Matthew's gospel and it ends Matthew's gospel when Jesus tells his apostles before his ascension "behold, I am with you always, to the end of the age."

One other lesson Joseph can teach us. He had an important job to do and it didn't get him much credit or recognition. Is it enough satisfaction just to know we've done our job and we've done it well without anyone praising us for it? If we can say "yes" to that, that's all that's important. When we think of Joseph today, we might think of all the wonderful people in our society and in our lives who, without a lot of fanfare, make good things happen and be grateful for them and grateful to God for giving them to us. I am certainly grateful for all the great and wonderful people who are here at St. Boniface and there are a lot of you. Amen.

Christmas
December 25, 2010

HOMILY – Each year Santa gets more than a million emails. These are a few that made me smile, compliments of *Reader's Digest* (Dec. 2010/Jan. 2011 pg 181). 1) from Christian age 7: "Mommy and daddy say I have not been very good these past few days. How bad can I be before I lose my presents?" 2) from Bri age 7: I'm sorry for putting all that Ex-lax in your milk last year, but I wasn't sure if you were real. My dad was really mad." 3) from Rosanne age 11: "Do you know Jesus is the real reason for Christmas? I don't want to hurt your feelings, but it's true."

I had time this week to read a number of inspiring stories about Christmas, stories that brought tears to my eyes, stories of unexpected gifts of kindness, children's Christmas pageants, Christmas miracles, finding the perfect Christmas tree, surviving Christmas after the loss of a loved one, funny stories, stories about faith and hope and, of course, love. I have often used one of those stories in my Christmas homily.

This year I feel inspired to focus on what is most central to Christmas and that is Jesus' birth. Four mini themes I want to share with you keep going around in my mind. The first theme is birthdays. When we celebrate them, when we send cards and give gifts, we are saying the person whose birthday we celebrate is important to us. They are a source of joy, and inspiration, a friend, they enrich us in some way. We don't know the exact day on which Jesus was born or even the exact year, although the year most scholars seem to agree on was 6 BC. It doesn't really matter; the important thing is that he was born; he came into this world as a tiny baby, not as a grown person, not as an alien from outer space. Though he was God, he took on our human nature, grew up as we all have to do, learning and helping at home. He prayed, he made friends, he worked for a living, he suffered misunderstanding, rejection, humiliation and death. He spoke to us in our own language and out of our own experience. He came to bring gifts to all who would have them, gifts we call grace, gifts of God's love and life. So on his birthday we offer him our thanks and praise, we gather together with family and friends to celebrate his birth, we send cards to one another rejoicing in his birth and we give gifts to one another following his inspiration of having given so much to us. His birthday is worth celebrating (not in immorality or drunkenness, gluttony, rivalry or jealousy as Paul says – Rom. 13:13) but in love and joy through the Holy Spirit.

The second theme: if we want to experience the real spirit of Christmas, then we have to look into our heart and discover what Jesus means to us: does he give us hope, forgiveness, peace; is his wisdom a guide for us through this life's journey; is he a companion to support us in lonely times, a friend we can thank when we know we've been blest; is he our God who died for us and who desires our obedience and our love. As with those who are our friends, do we feel drawn to make time to be with him. What does Jesus mean to us? That's what Christmas will mean to us. Christ has influenced our world more than any person who has ever been born. Does Jesus influence us in any profound way?

My third theme is about the manger. A manger is a trough or box for food for horses or cattle. St. Luke seems to focus on Jesus lying in a manger. The angel announced this is how the shepherds would identify their savior – he would be lying in a manger. Sometimes when we think about Jesus lying in a manger, we are distracted by the heartlessness of the innkeeper or the poverty of the holy family. Maybe the innkeeper was heartless when Joseph and Mary arrived and maybe the holy family had run out of money. The gospels don't tell us much about their finances. Joseph was a skilled craftsman after all and Herod loved having building projects – which would have provided employment for lots of people. It is likely though that the main issue Luke wants us to pay attention to is the manger. If we were to read this passage like a Jew would, we would be familiar with the beginning of the Book of Isaiah where Isaiah is scolding God's people for turning away from God. Isaiah said: "Sons have I raised and reared, but they have disowned me! An ox knows its owner and a donkey knows the manger of its master." In other words, Isaiah is saying even an animal knows who it belongs to and who will care for it, but God's people did not know. Now, with the shepherds, Luke is pointing out to us that Israel is beginning to find its Lord and when the shepherds found him they went out and shared with others the good news they had been told.

The manger leads to my fourth theme: the Eucharist. Jesus told us he is food for us, he is the bread of life. He could not have been more clear: "I am the living bread that came down from heaven; whoever eats this bread will live forever; and the bread that I will give is my flesh for the life of the world." It takes a big leap of faith to see in the small wafer no longer bread but the living power and presence of Jesus Christ, the Son of God. It took a great leap of faith for people to see divinity in Jesus. Christians today readily accept Jesus as divine but the big challenge to faith for us is to believe in the Eucharist. If the Son of God can become human then he can just as easily become our food and drink under the appearance of bread and wine. "Bethlehem" itself is translated as the "house of food." Christ is with us in many ways, through Scripture, through the least of his brothers and sisters, through the Church, but the Eucharist is the most pure and perfect way we connect with him and be nourished by him. If you are looking for him, "this will be a sign for you," you will find him in the spiritual food he gives us.

It is a blessing for me to celebrate with you Jesus' birth. I hope that from these thoughts you might take something with you to help you know why you should celebrate today. Amen.

Holy Family
December 30, 2007

HOMILY – (Sirach 3:3-7, 14-17a, Colossians 3:12-21, Matthew 2:13-15, 19-23) Just a few days ago we heard St. Luke describe the birth of Jesus at Bethlehem. Although the manger may not have been the Ritz, we imagined a scene described in the song: Silent night, Holy night. The silence of that night was broken only by the angels praising God and announcing peace to God's people on earth. Now we hear Matthew's gospel. The peace and quiet are gone. The paranoid king, Herod the Great, is intent on destroying the child Jesus and the Holy Family have to escape by leaving their own homeland and becoming refugees in neighboring Egypt. It's like a splash of cold water in the face, but this splash is really a splash of cold reality, reminding us that no family, not even the holiest has a stress-free existence. It also reminds us of the universal conflict and tension between the forces of good and evil, light and darkness, grace and sin. The forces of evil lined up against Jesus right from the beginning. Matthew's story also reminds us that although our decision to follow Jesus takes us along a road that leads to eternal happiness, that road is not always a paved or smooth.

Our focus today is on the family. The importance of the family cannot be overstated or over emphasized. The family is where we discover what it means to be human, what are our strengths and weaknesses, where we experience love and forgiveness, where we learn about relationships, unity, sacrifice, loving others, accepting others, where we learn values and attitudes and trust and how to handle stress and how to be responsible. Family is where we learn how to get along with one another. All these important learning tasks are hopefully learned in a family that is relatively healthy. I say "relatively healthy" because none of us and none of our families are perfect. A family that is seriously dysfunctional teaches a lot of other things that end up not being very helpful. The success of society depends depend on the health of the family. That creates a big burden for families to carry. It also puts a big burden on society to care about the family and to foster healthy families.

Today we celebrate the importance of another family, our parish family. Here too we discover who we are as God's children, how to trust God and to love God and one another. We learn values here too, values that are intended to lead us into eternal life. Hopefully we learn how to give as well as take, how to forgive as well as be forgiven. Here we gather around a family table to be fed, not with perishable food but with food that will nourish us eternally. Our faith community is just as important in its own way as our family of origin. And the Lord's supper that we share is just as important to our spiritual well being as being together and eating together as a family is to our emotional well being.

Today we celebrate 10 years as the united family of St. Boniface and St. Patrick. Back in 1853 St. Aloysius

was founded as the Catholic parish in North Side. It
didn't last as such. The area grew and there was not
always peace between the Irish and the Germans, so in
less than 10 years St. Aloysius became two parishes: St.
Boniface and St. Patrick. On December 29, 1991 we
formally became once again, a single parish. Since St.
Boniface was structurally the stronger of the two and
since St. Boniface had a school, St. Patrick parishioners
moved here and the move was a good one from
practically every aspect. Only a hand full of people that
I know of were unhappy about the merger. (We passed
out a booklet a few years ago which contains much more
history about our parish. Most people probably already
have one, but if you do not we have some more at the
doors of church.)

It has been my privilege to be pastor here for the ten
years since our merger. None of us knows what the future
holds, but if I could make a guess, I think for many
reasons St. Boniface will be here for a long time. As for
myself, if my health holds up and if the Archbishop lets
me I would like to be here for at least another six years.
By then I will be 70. I do not know what I will do when
I turn 70. I will have to reevaluate things when I get
there.

I do want to say how grateful I am to have so many
people's support. There's only one thing I wish, and that
is that more people took seriously the serious obligation
to attend Mass weekly. I think that for the most part
families are strengthened by meals together. And the
Lord's supper is our family meal each week. I have seen
too many people, once they get away from going to Mass
every week, slowly drift away from their faith. St. Paul
gives us a wonderful list of virtues that would enhance
and enrich any of our relationships with one another,
especially the relationships within our families:

compassion, kindness, gentleness, humility, patience, forgiveness, etc. Notice in this short passage he tells us twice to be grateful. The words St. Paul wrote of course were Greek, but you might find it instructive to hear what words he used: the verb he used was "Eucharisteo." And he tells us we are to become "Eucharistos." It is obvious from these words that the Eucharist allows us to perfectly fulfill his mandate. It is a perfect act of thanksgiving because, in a special way, we, as God's sons and daughters, offer thanks in union with God' own Son, Jesus Christ. May we, on this anniversary, give thanks for our family in Christ, and for our own immediate families. May we be strong and healthy families, full of thankfulness, and may we rejoice one day in the home of the one Father we all have in common, our Father in heaven. Amen.

Mary Mother of God
January 1, 2008

HOMILY – (Numbers 6:22-27, Galatians 4:4-7, Luke 2:16-21) We have an insatiable appetite for new things. We constantly ask one another "What's new?" The media makes big money keeping us up to date on the latest happenings, good or bad. We read catalogues or search the internet to find out what new things are out there. Some new things are worth celebrating: a new cure for cancer, a new car, a new outfit. Some new things we approach with guarded optimism: a new acquaintance, a new teacher, a new president; and some things are cause for no celebration at all: a new pain somewhere, a new bill we were not expecting.

Most everyone approaches the new year as a something worth celebrating. Perhaps it's as good an excuse for a party as anything else. Perhaps we know our new year's resolutions are going to make us into that kind of person we've always wanted to be. Or perhaps we're just glad we made it this far. There are any number of reasons people celebrate. At the same time, however, if we are realistic, we know each new year could bring new challenges, new dangers, new sadness, new tragedy. These are not things we want to think about and certainly not things to celebrate. They are things to pray about, and that's one good reason to begin the year right here, right where we are now: asking God's blessings for whatever is ahead.

Our first reading today is one that we are all familiar with as it is often used as our final blessing at Mass. It is a blessing by which Aaron the high priest, the brother of Moses, blessed God's people as they prepared for their journey to the Promised Land. They had been in the desert of Sinai now for a year. God had made a covenant with them and now they have detailed instructions on how to proceed on to the land of Israel, the Promised Land. Their expectations were high as they started out. Unfortunately the journey did not go well. They had the assurance of a close relationship with God, but they easily became dissatisfied with the hardships of their journey. They gave in to fear of what was ahead and complained they would rather be back in Egypt as slaves. The journey they were on required constant trust in God and they found that hard to do. Sometimes God is all we have to rely on.

The difficult moments of our lives call for trust as well. God is taking us on a journey into a new year, into a new chapter in our lives. If we proceed with trust, the journey will go more smoothly. We do have God's blessings on us.

God's blessing is not something we can see. The shepherds saw angels and the baby Jesus. The people of

Israel saw miracles after Jesus had grown up. The Apostles saw Jesus after he had risen. We have only a word to depend on, the word of Jesus: "I will be with you always." And we have the special sign of his presence in the Eucharist guaranteed by his word: "This is my body." "This is my blood." When the shepherds saw Jesus he probably looked pretty much like most any other little baby. They had only the word of the angels to believe he was special. Our host at Mass doesn't look like anything exceptional either, but Jesus' word tells us it is. It is our Lord and our God who nourishes us as we make our journey through life. This is our guarantee that we have God's blessing on us as we travel on. Having this assurance we who believe can celebrate as we begin a new year. May it be truly blessed for all of us. Amen.

Feast of the Epiphany
January 2, 2011

INTRODUCTION – Jerusalem was destroyed by the Babylonians 587 years before Christ. Fifty years later, the Persians (people living in modern day Iran) conquered the Babylonians, and they allowed the Jews to return home. They found their city and their homeland still in shambles. Rebuilding was extremely difficult. Today's prophet, whom we hear in our first reading, tries to encourage the people and assure them Jerusalem would again be a great city. He sees Jerusalem becoming the center of spirituality and light for all the world. People would come from everywhere to visit Jerusalem and to be nourished by the spiritual light and life radiating from it. St. Matthew sees this vision fulfilled in the birth of Jesus and the coming of the magi. Through Jesus, the message of God's love and salvation will radiate to all the world.

HOMILY – Happy New Year to everyone here! There was a cartoon in a publication I get with a man and his wife sitting by their Christmas tree. He was holding a book in his lap saying to her: "It's a nice gift, but I have mixed feelings about a leather-bound collection of my New Year's resolutions from the last twenty years." (*The Joyful Noiseletter*, Jan. 2005)

We've all gotten a year older and there are plenty of funny stories about aging. I'll just entertain you with one so I have a little time to talk about our gospel: A man was telling his friend: "I've sure gotten old! I've had two bypass surgeries, a hip replacement, new knees, fought diabetes and I'm half blind. I take 40 different medications that make me dizzy, winded and subject to blackouts. I have bouts with dementia, poor circulation, hardly feel my hands and feet anymore. Can't remember if I'm 85 or 92. Have lost all my friends. But, thank God, I still have my driver's license." (from an email) Remember this in the new year: "You don't stop laughing because you grow old, you grow old because you stop laughing."

Today's gospel is one of the most popular stories in the Bible and rightly so. It recognizes the essence of the gospel story that God has made himself present to us in the person of Jesus, God's only Son, God from God, light from light, true God from true God, one in being with the Father. Previously in Matthew's gospel, Matthew told us another name for Jesus would be Emmanuel, "God with us."

The revelation that Jesus was Son of God is offensive to some, a contradiction to others, but it is salvation for those who believe in Jesus. The magi are the forerunners of those who would come to believe in Jesus, the first of those people foreseen by the prophet 500 years before Christ who would come to Jerusalem seeking the light of

God's glory. The magi are the first of those who would do homage to Jesus who would in a few short years be made known to all nations through the preaching of the apostles.

In the Book of Numbers (the fourth book of the Bible) there is a story of the Jews on their way to the Promised Land, under the leadership of Moses, after their liberation from their slavery in Egypt. On their way, they had to pass through the land of Moab, the area just east of the Dead Sea. The king of Moab hired a famous soothsayer from the East, a man named Balaam, to come and lay a curse on the Israelites. Balaam would have been a kind of magi, for that's what magi did. They were practiced in the occult arts: astronomers, fortunetellers and magicians with preternatural powers. It's an interesting story of how his donkey saw an angel blocking the way and the donkey refused to go on. Balaam beat his donkey and the donkey spoke to him. Then Balaam saw the angel and asked forgiveness. Eventually Balaam got to Moab and could see the Israelites from a mountain, but he couldn't curse them. Every time he tried to speak he could only speak a blessing. Among his oracles, Balaam saw a king who would come from Israel, whose royalty would be exalted. He said: "I see him, though not now; I behold him, though not near: A star shall advance from Jacob, and a staff shall rise from Israel." Balaam's oracle was later seen to apply to King David who would not reign until almost 300 years later (thus: "I behold him, though not now.") Later Judaism saw this as a reference to the Messiah.

The magi who visited Jesus when he was born, in seeing the star of the King of the Jews at its rising, were to "behold him, but not now." His kingship would not be proclaimed until he had hung on the cross beneath the title The King of the Jews, and had been raised up to be seated at the right hand of the Father in the resurrection.

Already we see in today's readings those who should have embraced his reign as either indifferent to him, such as the chief priests, or seriously threatened by him, such as Herod. Yet, in spite of opposition, people have always given him homage and always will, for as the angel announced to Mary, of his kingdom there will be no end. Amen.

Baptism of the Lord
January 9, 2011

INTRODUCTION – The words of the prophet Isaiah, in today's first reading, go back 500 years before Christ. This passage was intended for the Jews who were in exile in Babylon. God is, through the prophet, introducing a person referred to only as God's servant to his people. God is quite pleased with his servant. In a non-violent way, God's servant will establish justice in the world, be a light to the nations and liberation for captives. Scholars debate who this servant might have been 500 years before Christ, but with the coming of Christ, there is no doubt who is God's perfect servant. At Jesus' baptism, God introduces Jesus to the world, not just as his servant, but as his beloved Son with whom he is well-pleased.

HOMILY – If you struggle to understand the baptism of Jesus, you're not alone. Even John the Baptist had difficulty understanding why Jesus came to him for baptism. As John said "I need to be baptized by you, and yet you are coming to me?"

The baptism of Jesus is a mystery worthy of our contemplation. Certainly Pope John Paul considered it as something worth meditating on when he made it one of the mysteries in the new set of mysteries he created for the rosary: the luminous mysteries or the mysteries of light.

When Carol Roosa was taking a course at the Athenaeum to become our pastoral administrator, she had to present a paper on the topic of baptism. The professor was quite impressed with it and so she volunteered to preach this Sunday. I said "no." She said it would only take an hour and fifteen minutes. You will be happy to know I stood my ground. Besides, only priests and deacons are allowed to do a homily. I say all of this to illustrate there is so much that could be said about baptism. I'm not going to say it all. My few words today will, I hope, throw a little light on the sacrament of baptism and might help make the baptism of Jesus a little more understandable.

First I want to point out one way in which the baptism of Jesus by John was totally different from our sacrament of baptism. Then I want to mention one way in which they are similar.

If I were to ask the average Catholic what they think of when they hear the word baptism, most would answer, "Baptism takes away original sin." That's true, but there is a better answer. Let me illustrate. (show wallet) Now many of you know what this is: a wallet. And it's empty, and some of you might relate to that too. That's basically what original sin is. It is emptiness, like this wallet. It's a big nothing. We are empty of God's grace and life. Suppose, for example, by some unbelievable odds, I would win a million dollars in the lottery. I would get that big check (less taxes) and put it in the wallet. If someone were to ask me, "what's in your wallet?," I don't know what I would tell them, but I don't think I would answer "the emptiness in my wallet is gone." But that's what we say when we define baptism as the sacrament that takes away original sin. That definition only emphasizes the emptiness and not the fullness. It doesn't reflect the blessings that suddenly fill us at baptism: the blessings of God's life, of being children of God, the blessings of the Holy Spirit, the blessing of belonging to the family of God, the blessing and hope of sharing in eternal happiness with God. In Jesus there was no emptiness. In him dwells the fullness of the divinity (Col. 2:9) as St. Paul tells us. He was, from all eternity, God's beloved Son. Jesus had no need of baptism in any form. In this respect Jesus' baptism by John made no change in him as the sacrament of baptism did for us. Jesus' baptism by John provides an occasion for us to reflect on our own baptism and the grace that it brought us.

Now I want to describe one way in which Jesus' baptism by John and the sacrament of baptism we received are similar. They are similar in that they are both a commitment. John's baptism was a public commitment people made to live holy lives and to prepare for the coming of God's kingdom. Jesus, in being baptized, was publicly committing himself to do God's will and to preach and build the kingdom of God. Baptism is that for us too. We are committed, in a public event, to belong to God, to be God's obedient child, God's lover, God's representative. It's something like declaring one's candidacy, not for public office, but for the office of Christian in the world. Most likely someone made that commitment for us, most probably our parents. They made that commitment for us with the intention of directing us in God's ways. Eventually, we have to make that commitment our own if our baptism is going to mean anything at all. On this feast of the baptism of Jesus, we have a good opportunity to recommit ourselves to Jesus. The effects and blessings of baptism remain with us as long as we do not turn our hearts away from the Father who long ago chose us to be his son or daughter in the sacrament. In this way Jesus' baptism by John is very much like our own, not a private, secret event but a public, open declaration of our commitment to love and serve God and others as Jesus, the perfect Son of God did. Amen.

Second Sunday in Ordinary Time
January 16, 2011

INTRODUCTION – (Is 49:3, 5-6; 1 Cor. 1:1-3; Jn. 1:29-34) Last week, in our first reading, we heard about God's servant who would bring justice and light to the world. We hear again about God's servant leading the people of Israel back to God, and bringing God's salvation to the ends of the earth. These passages about God's servant (there are four of them) were written over 500 years before Christ. Scholars do not know exactly who might have fit the description of God's servant at that time, but with the advantage of hindsight we see how perfectly the servant songs describe God's perfect servant, Jesus Christ.

HOMILY – One weekend, a doctor, a priest and an attorney were out in a fishing boat. Their motor had died and one of their oars had been dropped in the water and was drifting off. Just as the doctor was about to dive in to retrieve the oar, the boat was surrounded by sharks. Suddenly the doctor changed his mind and said, "I can't jump in now. Someone might get bitten and they'll need my medical services." The priest said "I can't go. If the doctor suffered a fatal bite, I would have to give him the last rites." "Fine," said the attorney, "I'll get the oar," and he dove in. The sharks moved away, he retrieved the oar and got back into the boat. The doctor and the priest were flabbergasted. The attorney just smiled and said, "Professional courtesy."

What does that have in common with the gospel? Other than my simply wanting to tell it for a long time, it doesn't have much connection with the gospel, except someone had to have the courage to put their life on the line, which Jesus did, and the sharks didn't get out of the way for him because they were out to get him.

Today's gospel does not tell us who the Baptist was addressing when he gave his testimony about Jesus. Perhaps it's us he is talking to. He begins by telling us Jesus is "the Lamb of God who takes away the sin of the world." The image of "lamb" was a very rich image for the Jews. It spoke of the paschal lamb that was sacrificed at Passover and was the main part of the Passover dinner when the Jews celebrated their liberation from slavery and their special covenant with God. It could also refer to the servant of God whom Isaiah writes about who was led like a lamb to the slaughter or a sheep before the shearers in his passion. (Is. 53:7) Any of these concepts could apply to Jesus.

The Baptist said Jesus was "the Lamb of God who takes away the sin of the world." Notice the word "sin." When we recite or sing the "lamb of God" before Communion, we say he takes away the "sins" of the world. The singular word "sin" is used as a description of the general state the world finds itself in. Poverty, war, injustice, hatred, dishonesty, killings, sexual perversion, greed, unnecessary suffering, etc. Our sins (plural) are expressions of our participation in the sinful environment we live in. On the other hand, our good actions are expressions of the kingdom of God Christ came to establish. I just had a long discussion with a friend who couldn't understand how Christ frees us from sin. This is a major area of study in theology which I cannot get into today. Thinking back on the conversation I had with my friend, it struck me that part of our difficulty in understanding how Christ saved us from sin is that we tend not to see how sin affects us, to what extent it is part of the world we live in, and how we participate in it. It's like living in a bubble. A bubble is invisible to those who live inside it. People have experienced this with the technology bubble and more recently with the real estate bubble. Jesus came to us that by his life and teaching, his death and resurrection, he could lead us from a world of sin into God's kingdom, where there would be no more suffering or sadness or evil of any kind and where we would know peace, love and joy for all eternity.

Last week when Jesus came to be baptized, we heard the Baptist tell Jesus, "I need to be baptized by you and yet you are coming to me?" Today the Baptist gives testimony to that event. He saw the Spirit come down on Jesus and remain on him. I think the Baptist thought he knew Jesus and knew Jesus was holier than he was, that's why he didn't feel worthy to baptize Jesus. But through the signs that took place when Jesus was baptized, the Baptist came to know Jesus much more profoundly: that he was the one to take away the sin of the world, the one to initiate God's kingdom, the one who would baptize with the Holy Spirit. So he could say in truth, "I did not know him." John realized his mission to prepare for Jesus' coming, was now to make him known to Israel which, if we read the passages that follow today's reading, we will see him doing.

I was thinking this morning of those who had the role of the Baptist in my life, my parents, teachers, my confessor, the members of the Third Order of St. Francis, and the many dedicated lay people I have met in my ministry. I have probably been influenced as much or even more by wonderful faith-filled lay people than I have been by clerics and religious. I'm not putting down religious vocations because religious have definitely touched my life, but I mention the importance of lay people because we all are called to make Christ known to others, and my faith would not be half of what it is without their influence.

And so, the Baptist gives his testimony about Jesus to us today. May we not be shy in sharing our faith in Jesus with others. Amen.

Third Sunday in Ordinary Time
January 23, 2011

INTRODUCTION – (Isaiah 8:23-9:3; 1 Corinthians 1:10-13,17; Matthew 4:12-23) Galilee is located about 75 miles north of Jerusalem. With cars and expressways, that's not very far at all. Since most people traveled on foot at the time of Jesus, it took a few days to make a 75 mile trip. Consequently, Galilee was often forgotten or looked down upon by the religious leaders in Jerusalem. Seven hundred years before Christ, the Assyrians conquered Galilee. Those Jews they didn't kill were sent into exile. The Assyrians did this to all nations they conquered, thus preventing conquered nations from regrouping and rebelling against them. The Assyrians moved a lot of pagans into Galilee to replace the Jews they exiled. In Jesus' time, seven hundred years later, there were still a lot of pagans living there as well as Jews who had moved back, so the population was pretty well mixed.

The prophet Isaiah, who was living in Jerusalem at the time the Assyrians conquered Galilee, foresaw good things for that area in spite of all the devastation the

Galileans suffered. Isaiah said a great light would shine upon Galilee that would bring them abundant joy. If our first reading from Isaiah sounds familiar, it's probably because we just heard it a month ago. It was part of our first reading on Christmas. St. Matthew, in today's gospel, tells us Jesus' ministry in Galilee was the fulfillment of Isaiah's prophecy. It would have been normal for a religious teacher like Jesus to do his preaching and teaching mainly in Jerusalem. (*Joachim Jeremias* pg 242) Jesus, however, chose to begin his ministry in Galilee. In these readings Galilee is called by the names of two of the tribes of Israel that originally settled there: Zebulun and Naphtali.

HOMILY – A U.S. Congressman died and went to heaven. "Welcome," said St. Peter. "We seldom see Congressmen here." Then St. Peter explained, "This is how things work here. You'll spend one day in hell and one day in heaven, and then you will have to choose where you want to spend eternity." When the Congressman went to hell, he saw a golf course, clubhouse, and politician friends. They dined and reminisced. Their host, the devil, seemed very pleasant. The next day the Congressman returned to heaven where he saw many contented souls playing musical instruments and singing. "It's time to choose eternity," St. Peter said. The Congressman reflected and chose hell. Back in hell, the Congressman saw a barren land full of garbage, fire and smoke, and his friends in rags. A smiling devil greeted him. The Congressman protested, "yesterday there was golf, lobster, champagne, and great times. What happened?" The devil replied, "yesterday we were campaigning, today you voted." (from *The Joyful Noiseletter*, June-July 2008, pg. 2) Be sure to vote for heaven. I think the devil, the father of lies as Jesus calls him, tries to convince people not that hell is fun, but that there is no such place. If that were true, then all of Jesus' warnings and work to bring us into God's kingdom would be meaningless – if we're all going to end up there anyway!

Today we hear the beginning of Jesus' public ministry. Some scholars believe that originally Jesus was a follower of John the Baptist. Eventually the Baptist allowed Jesus to work independently, preaching and baptizing in the southern part of Israel near Judea while the Baptist moved north into Galilee. Then when Herod Antipas put John in prison, which is a long story in itself, Jesus replaced him in Galilee. St. Matthew sees this as a fulfillment of the prophet Isaiah that the people in Galilee will see a great light. Matthew tells us Jesus began his teaching with the same message of John the Baptist: "Repent, for the kingdom of heaven is at hand." Proclaiming the coming of the kingdom of heaven or the kingdom of God is a basic mission if not the basic mission of Jesus. This year in Cycle A we hear mostly from St. Matthew's gospel and we will notice that Matthew prefers to use the expression, "the kingdom of heaven," whereas the other three Gospels use the phrase, "the kingdom of God." Both phrases mean the same thing. It could be that Matthew was being extra-sensitive about not using the word God. Jews never spoke God's name and Matthew seems to be going even further and chooses almost all the time to say the kingdom of heaven. Another word for kingdom would be rule or reign, so whenever we hear the phrase "the kingdom of heaven," Jesus is talking about the reign of God. Exactly what that means is not easy to define in a few words. It refers more to an action: that God is ruling powerfully as King. This is by far an oversimplification but it will help us understand it a little better if we consider four major principles that characterize it: 1) there are good and evil forces in the world, 2) the evil forces rule the present time, 3) God will intervene in a powerful way in history, overthrow the forces of evil and establish his good kingdom and 4) the kingdom is imminent.

We need to point out that God is not a fearsome, remote deity but a divine king who delights in being a loving father, a father who rejoices over gathering his lost children to himself. This concept of the coming reign of God is reflected in all that Jesus did and taught. Another word for this expectation of God reclaiming God's rightful place in the world as its ruler and savior is apocalyptic. In this sense Jesus is an apocalyptic preacher/prophet who not only calls us to repent and prepare for the kingdom which is near but who also brings this kingdom into existence.

Right away Jesus begins to gather those who would help him in this work. All of them are not named in today's passage, but the number 12 is important. Remember there were 12 patriarchs who fathered the twelve tribes of Israel. This symbolizes that Jesus is establishing a new Israel, the new people of God who would be faithful to God. Notice that Jesus is not one of the 12. He is over and above all his 12 apostles and over the entire kingdom he has come to proclaim. In time Jesus needed more than 12 special leaders to help him proclaim the coming of God's good kingdom and God's love. Jesus still needs people to help share in that work. He even told us to pray that the Lord of the harvest would send workers into his harvest. Our Archbishop has asked each parish to pray weekly for this intention. For a few years now we have been praying the prayer of Pope John Paul II for vocations at our holy hours. Following the desire of our Lord and of our Archbishop that we pray for vocations, I am going to pray this prayer after the Communion prayer. Soon we will have copies of the prayer for everyone so that you can all join in.

When it came time for Jesus to leave this world, he said he would return in glory. People throughout the ages have anticipated when this might be. Throughout the past 2000 years, as often as someone predicted when Jesus would return, they have been wrong. The latest expectation is that the Mayan calendar is supposed to tell us the world will end on 12/21/2012. Jesus told us no one knows. He told us to not go running around looking for it to happen for it will come when we least expect it. What we need to do is to believe that God's good kingdom will triumph in the end. We will share in that victory if we stay close to Jesus and if we are always prepared.

4th Sunday in Ordinary Time
January 30, 2011

INTRODUCTION – (Zephaniah 2:3; 3:12-13, 1 Corinthians 1: 26-31, Matthew 5: 1-12a) The day of the Lord would be a day of liberation for God's people and a day of judgment for God's enemies and the enemies of God's people. It would be a day of doom and destruction or a day of joy. It all depended where a person stood with God. It didn't matter whether a person belonged to the "chosen people," what did matter is how they lived. Our first reading is from the prophet Zephaniah who lived during a time of colossal change and shifts of world power. Assyria's hold on the Middle East was crumbling and Babylon was swiftly asserting its strength and would soon destroy Assyria. The long 50 plus year reign of Manasseh had just ended with his death. As king in Jerusalem and descendant of David, he brought into the Temple pagan worship, human sacrifice and sacred prostitution. His son, Amon, was assassinated after two years and so his son Josiah was installed as king at the age of eight. Josiah led a reform that brought people back to the God of Israel. As you can see, it was a time of great upheaval during the time of Zephaniah. It is a short reading telling us in the first verse "perhaps" those who are humble and who observe God's law would survive the day of the Lord's anger. The rest of the passage is God's promise to bless the humble and the lowly who take refuge in him.

HOMILY – A wealthy man, who rarely went to church, was on his deathbed and sent for the pastor. "Pastor," he said, "you know I've never cared much for church matters but I'm about to die, and I want to be sure of my eternal salvation. Do you suppose that if I gave $1 million to the church, and $100,000 to you personally, I would go to heaven?" The pastor thought about that idea for a second or two and then replied, "well, sir, I can't say for sure, but what do you have to lose? It's worth a try!" (*Joyful Noiseletter*, February, 2005, pg. 2)

If that had been me I would love to have been able to say that would work for the man for sure, but in all honesty I would have had to answer like the pastor in the story. Our Lord expects more from us. Today we begin the Sermon on the Mount where Jesus begins to lay out what he does expect of us. The Sermon on the Mount is the first of five major sections of St. Matthew's gospel dedicated to Jesus' teachings. It is not necessarily a sermon Jesus preached from beginning to end. It is made up of many things Jesus taught on other occasions, which Matthew chose, as the writer of the gospel, to put together in this form as one sermon. I want to stress this is one of five sections Matthew gives us of Jesus' teaching; thus this one sermon is not everything Jesus taught. Matthew makes a point of Jesus preaching on a mountain. He seeks to present Jesus as a new Moses, who proclaimed God's law to God's people on a mountain.

However, Jesus is greater than Moses proclaiming a new and greater law from the source of divine revelation.

Last week we heard Jesus in the gospel calling people to "repent, for the kingdom of heaven is at hand." Remember "kingdom of heaven" means "reign of God." It was an apocalyptic message. The apocalyptic viewpoint is that God would come in some cataclysmic way at some future time to bring judgment and punishment on those who live evil lives and to bring reward to those who live good lives. It is essentially the "Day of the Lord" I spoke of before the first reading. The beatitudes are part of that apocalyptic message. Those who are poor in spirit are those who recognize their own weakness, their own dependence, their own indebtedness to God for everything. In other words, those who are humble and who know how much they need God, theirs is the kingdom of heaven (partially now – fully in the future). Those who think they can make it through life without God will, unhappily, get what they desire – having to continually make it on their own without God (unless they repent). Those who mourn will have things turned around for them and their sorrow will be turned into joy. The meek and those who hunger and thirst for righteousness (holiness) will have their needs met. The merciful, the clean of heart, the peacemakers will be rewarded and those persecuted for their good lives will gain the kingdom. God will turn the tables on everyone someday, whenever that day of the Lord comes.

"Apocalypse" means "revelation." Jesus is, as he begins his ministry, revealing what is to be. What is to be is that God will be faithful to those who desire him and who are faithful to him. The disciple who is mourning or who is being persecuted or who is crying out for God's help may not feel especially blessed; but he or she is blessed because they have God's loving presence and consolation with them now, and they have the hope of the blessedness to come. To be part of the kingdom God offers us, we must prepare as we heard Jesus say last week. We must do the things he has asked of us, things we will hear as we read further in the Sermon on the Mount over the next several weeks. We gather together now in prayer trusting in him who invites us to follow him into God's kingdom. Amen.

Presentation of the Lord
February 2, 2003

INTRODUCTION – (Malachi 3:1-4; Hebrews 2:14-18; Luke 2:22-40) Today's feast is difficult to understand unless you know about a couple of Jewish laws. The first law you need to know about is that every first born male, whether it was a person or an animal was considered as belonging in a special way to God. You will find this written in the book of Exodus. If it was a male animal that was born, it was offered up as a sacrifice. If it was a baby boy, a sacrifice was offered for the child.

The second Old Testament law we need to look at is in Leviticus. It stated that when a woman gave birth to a baby she was not permitted to participate in Temple worship for 40 days. After 40 days she had to go through a service of purification and offer a sacrifice so she would be admitted to public worship again. This explains why this feast is celebrated 40 days after Christmas.

Besides knowing about these two laws, the first reading from the prophet Malachi could use a little background explanation. The time is after the Babylonian exile was over and the Jews had returned to their homeland. They built a modest temple to replace the Temple of Solomon that the Babylonians destroyed. The Jews were negligent in their religious responsibilities. Their worship was sloppy and lacking in sincerity. Their attitude toward God's laws was very lax. The people were in need of someone who would bring them back to a true love for God, back to obedience of God and back to sincere worship. The prophet foretold that God himself, in his love for his people, would come to his Temple to cleanse and purify his people and make them truly good and holy. Luke sees the Presentation in the Temple as a fulfillment of Malachi's prophecy. It is truly the Lord who comes to the Temple when Jesus is brought there by Mary and Joseph. But we see such irony here. As a humble servant of God Mary comes to be purified, she who is "full of grace." And according to the Law, she and Joseph offer a sacrifice, but their son, Jesus, would eliminate the need for any future animal sacrifices, since he would give his life as a perfect sacrifice that will save the whole world.

HOMILY – Why should Mary be purified and a sacrifice be offered? St. Luke tells us it is because Joseph and Mary were in every way faithful to their religion. Notice how many times St. Luke speaks of Joseph and Mary fulfilling the law of the Lord.

The canticle of the holy man Simeon is a prayer that is prayed as part of Night Prayer by all who pray the divine office. It is a beautiful prayer for nighttime: "Now Lord you can dismiss your servant…" In this prayer, St. Luke is telling us that Jesus came to save all people: Christ would reveal his light to the Gentiles. St. Luke hints of the cross that is ahead for Mary and her child: "and you yourself a sword will pierce," Simeon tells Mary. St. Luke was very sensitive about gender. So often when he tells one of Jesus' parables about a man, he follows it up with one about a woman. Or if he tells us about Jesus healing a man, he immediately tells us about an occasion when Jesus healed a woman. Here too, he introduced Simeon to us, then he tells us about Anna. In Anna, we have a good example of an evangelist. After she saw Jesus, she "spoke about the child to all who were awaiting the redemption of Jerusalem." You don't have to be a priest or religious to tell others about Jesus. All you have to do is to be excited about God's saving love given to us in Jesus Christ.

I would like you to consider how Simeon and Anna recognized Jesus. I'm sure he looked like many other little babies who had been brought to the Temple over the ages. How did they know this was the one? Well, St. Luke tells us they were guided by the Holy Spirit and that would have been necessary. But he tells us also they were holy people. They were close to God and spent a lot of time with God in the Temple. I think it's like anything else. When I walk down the street I see trees. Maybe I might recognize a maple or an oak or a sycamore but most trees are just trees. I hear different kinds of birds, but I don't recognize any specific bird call or melody. A person who has studied biology or botany is much more aware of the many types of living creatures and plants that surround us. A person who has studied music can get much more out of Bach or Beethoven than I can. A person who has studied medicine is more able to recognize signs of health or sickness. If we are really close to someone, we can discern their moods better than a stranger can. Consequently the closer we are to God, the more aware we are of God's presence in our everyday lives. Simeon and Anna could see with the eyes of their minds and hearts what human eyes could not see. That's how they knew Jesus was the one. Do we want to see what our eyes cannot see, do we want to have a greater awareness of God's presence and his love, do we want to see the goodness and holiness in ourselves and in others? It's not hard to do. The way is to draw closer to our Lord. The better we know him, the more visible he will be to us. And the Holy Spirit will be there to help. Let us ask our Lord to help us recognize him now in prayer and sacrament as we continue with Mass.

5th Sunday in Ordinary Time
February 6, 2011

INTRODUCTION – (Isaiah 58:7-10; 1 Corinthians 2:1-5; Matthew 5:13-16) I speak of the Babylonian exile frequently because it was such an important part of Israel's history and because so many of the Old Testament writings were recorded shortly before or after that event. The people who survived the Babylonian destruction of Jerusalem and the territory around Jerusalem were in exile for 50 years until the Persians conquered the Babylonians and allowed God's people to return home. Most of those Jews who returned to Israel were the grandchildren of the ones who were taken into exile. When they got home to Israel, they found their cities and farms in a worse state than they were 50 years earlier after the Babylonians had conquered them. They had to rebuild everything, their farms, their homes, their businesses, their cities, their temple. Here is where our first reading comes in. Their efforts to survive created deep division in the community. It was survival of the fittest, and the poor and homeless were ignored. God is telling them that their selfish, self-centered, 'every man for himself' attitude was not going to be successful. If they wanted to grow and thrive, they had to start caring about each other. Justice, fairness, honesty and kindness would bring light into their darkness. Selfishness would bring continued suffering.

HOMILY – One Sunday the preacher's sermon went on endlessly. A man got up and walked out of the church. He came back near the end of the service. The pastor made an effort to greet him as the people were leaving church and said, "Clarence, I noticed you left during my sermon and then came back later. Are you feeling okay?" "Sure," Clarence said. "I'm okay. I just went out to get a haircut." "Why didn't you do that before you came to church?" The pastor asked. Clarence replied, "I didn't need it then." (*The Joyful Noiseletter*, Aug.-Sept. 2010, pg 2)

I'll bet few ever got up to leave while Jesus was speaking. He even had to work a miracle to feed the crowd because their day with Jesus lasted so long. Today's gospel from St. Matthew is a continuation of Jesus' Sermon on the Mount.

Some scripture passages could keep me talking for an hour and I struggle to keep my remarks within a reasonable timeframe. In today's readings the message is so clear that it is hardly necessary to say anything more about it, but a couple of points deserve a comment. As the Sermon on the Mount continues, Jesus tells us "you are the salt of the earth ... you are the light of the world." He wasn't just talking to his 12 apostles but to a large crowd. That includes us for the Scriptures are meant to teach us as well as those for whom they were originally written.

Jesus tells us we are the salt of the earth and the light of the world. To be light for the world is an obvious compliment for light is so important to us. Try to imagine a world in darkness. I wouldn't want to live in such a world. Even during these winter days when the days are short and it's cloudy and gloomy, some people are seriously affected. The condition is called S.A.D.

(seasonal affective disorder) and people who suffer from it become very depressed. To be called the "Salt of the earth" is also a high compliment, although today we are told to avoid the stuff as much as possible. At the time of Jesus, it was a very important commodity, primarily because it was a preservative. Without salt, food would spoil.

In praising us Jesus is also challenging us. In praising us he's telling us we have talents and gifts that could be of great value and help to others, talents and gifts we often do not give ourselves credit for. He also challenges us to be the gift to others that we can be. Our first reading from Isaiah describes how we can be light and salt for the world. Sometimes we are called to do big things to help others and sometimes it's the little day-to-day acts of kindness that are significant and important. Sometimes just giving another person a smile is all we need to do (and maybe the hardest thing for us to do).

Whatever we do to help another is going to bring blessings back to us. I'm sure we've all experienced that. I'd like to end with a quote from Patch Adams, a Doctor about whom a movie was made several years ago. He is also a doctor who likes to play the clown and bring humor into his healing work. He said "hugely important is the way a person expresses thanks for being alive. The person who does so through service will possess a great comfort throughout life."

We ask the Lord to bless us today as we come before him who is the source of all light, all wisdom and all blessings. Amen.

6th Sunday in Ordinary Time
February 13, 2011

INTRODUCTION – (Sirach 15:15-20; 1 Corinthians 2:6-10; Matthew 5:17-37) About a month ago I had to get a new computer. All my programs needed to be updated and it has been a challenge getting familiar with new technology. Sometimes my computer seems to have a mind of its own, but I know it really doesn't. I just need to get to know what I'm supposed to do and not supposed to do to get it to work like I want it to. Life's like that too. According to the first book of the Bible, the Book of Genesis, when God created human beings he gave us instructions about what we could and could not do, and his instructions weren't all that complicated. But, according to Genesis, our first parents thought they were smarter than God and decided to make up their own rules. They found out that was a disaster. Our first reading today, from Ben Sirach, is a reflection on sin and our freedom to choose right or wrong. Some of the philosophers of Ben Sirach's time (about 180 years before Christ) were teaching that "when I sin it's God who makes me do it." The author tells us that's not so. We have a free will and are able to choose right from wrong.

HOMILY – A young man was pouring over the selection of Valentine's Day cards at a local gift shop. The clerk asked if she could help. "I'm looking for your most beautiful Valentine card," he explained. "Something that expresses my deepest feelings." The clerk went to a section of cards and pulled out one that was beautifully embossed, trimmed with lace, and written in an elegant script. "This is a lovely card," she said and read the inside. "To my one true love, the light of my life, the joy of my heart, the very essence of beauty and grace. I love you more than I can say." The young man was thrilled. "That's perfect!" He said. "That's exactly what I'm looking for. I'll take five." (from www.ConnectionsMediaWorks.com: Feb. 2011, pg. 2)

We are full of contradictions and sometimes we really make a fool of ourselves. Sometimes things are humorous and sometimes they can get us into big trouble. As we know, the scribes and Pharisees of Jesus' day were often full of contradictions and self-deceit, convinced they were the truly holy ones and everyone else were great sinners. Jesus tells us if we want to enter the kingdom of God, we have to be better than they were. This week and next he gives us various illustrations of what he means by being better. Basically, he is trying to show us holiness goes beyond external behavior. Holiness must be deep inside of us – that which must be deep inside of us, that which makes us truly holy is love: love for God and love for each other.

Please don't misunderstand me. Certainly the way we behave is important. God's commandments tell us that. Thou shalt not kill, thou shalt not commit adultery, thou shalt not bear false witness, honor thy father and thy mother, keep holy the Lord's day, etc. We might feel like killing someone, but we don't do it. Keeping God's instructions about what we must do or not do will guide us to a better life. Jesus wants us also to have such love in our hearts that we not only do not kill others, but that we love them enough that we don't want to kill them; that we not only don't take our neighbor's wife, but that we love our neighbor and our own spouse, if we're married, to the extent that we don't even desire intimate relations with someone we're not married to. With technology and pornography it's really easy to fall into that trap today. He tells us also that not only should we not swear falsely, our love and respect for others should move us to always be truthful to anyone to whom we speak.

We might be thinking "that's a big order." Truly it is. Jesus asks a lot from his followers. Sirach tells us in the first reading, "if you choose, you can keep the commandments." We must add "only with God's help," for God is love and only with his help, a help that is available to us through prayer and the sacraments, can we be like him. As Jesus said, "without me you can do nothing."

We must be careful not to condemn ourselves when feelings come to us, feelings of anger, laziness, envy, lust, greed, pride or whatever. We are all human and we all experience those feelings. We would have to cut out our brain to eliminate feelings such as these. The important thing is, what do we do with these feelings, do we dwell on them, hold on to them, allow them to take over our thinking, or do we consider whether they fit with what Jesus would want of us and choose to go in the direction of what we know he would want.

This is a slightly different topic, but it's worth noting here the way Jesus taught. Jesus said "you have heard it was said ..." When the ordinary Jew learned God's law, it was read to them or preached to them (since owning a book then was a luxury). Then Jesus said "but I say to you ..." Jewish rabbi's never preached that way. Jesus is speaking here with great authority, an authority seemingly equal to God who originally gave us the Ten Commandments. People have often asked me whether he knew he was God. Right from the beginning of his ministry, it is obvious he didn't have any hesitancy about acting as if he were.

Today at our Mass of the Four Chaplains, we celebrate God's love shown to us in Jesus who taught us to love and who showed us perfect love through his own sacrifice to save us. We also today honor four men of God whose hearts and lives were filled with God's love.

Jesus said, "No one has greater love than this, that he lay down his life for his friends." (Jn. 15:13) Their sacrifice moves us beyond words and they remind us of the many men and women who also made great sacrifices for our safety and freedom, whose acts of love and service may never be known.

7th Sunday in Ordinary Time
February 20, 2011

INTRODUCTION – (Leviticus 19:1-2, 17-18; 1 Corinthians 3:16-23; Matthew 5:38-48) Our first reading is from Leviticus, the third book of the Bible. It has many laws about Old Testament priesthood and Temple sacrifices, but its central message is a call to holiness for all God's people. If you look up this portion of the book of Leviticus you will see that this call to holiness includes the Ten Commandments as well as a number of other commandments – all of which are summed up in the commandment to love one's neighbor as oneself. Jesus expands on this command in today's gospel, a continuation of his Sermon on the Mount.

HOMILY – Late one night, a truck driver pulled into a roadside café for a little something to eat. As he was eating, three nasty-looking motorcyclists noisily strutted in and made their way to the bar. For some unknown reason they gravitated toward the truck driver. One poured a little salt on his head, another knocked his pie on the floor and the third managed to knock the trucker's coffee off the counter and into the man's lap. The truck driver got up, said nothing, paid his bill and made his exit. "That dude sure wasn't much of a fighter" sneered one of the cyclists. The waiter peered out the window onto the dark parking lot and answered, "He's not much of a driver either. He just ran over three motorcycles." (*Sunday Homily Helps*, St. Anthony Messenger Press, for February 20, 2011) .

It gives joy to our hearts to see nasty people get paid back for their nastiness. Jesus gives us a different way to look at things in today's gospel. In last week's portion of the Sermon on the Mount, we heard Jesus list several of the commandments with the phrase, "you have heard that it was said ..." and then give us his interpretation of how we were to observe them with the words, "but I say to you ..." Today's gospel continues this pattern with two other commandments: the first is the law of talion, "an eye for an eye and a tooth for a tooth." The second is the law about love of neighbor.

Let's look briefly at each of these two commandments in today's gospel. The law of talion regards proportionate recompense. It is a very ancient principle shared by all civilized people. It is a principle on which we supposedly base our own legal system in that if someone harms you, any restitution must be proportionate to the harm done. When Jesus tells us not to resist one who is evil, he is not addressing those who have responsibility to keep order in society such as law enforcement officers and judges. Their job is to vindicate the rights of the injured. Without someone to keep order in society, there would only be chaos. Jesus is addressing the injured person himself or herself. He is not expressing it as a hard and fast rule that we have to allow ourselves to let other people walk all over us. Remember when Jesus was arrested and put on trial. When someone struck him on the cheek, he didn't turn the other cheek. He didn't retaliate either. He responded, "why did you strike me?" We are entitled to stand up for ourselves, but Jesus wants us to let love guide us rather than vengeance. If in society we always exact retribution every time we are injured or offended, we would all be going around blind and toothless as the Rev. Martin Luther King said. If all of us had to get even for every hurt in life, we would all end up hating one another. Sometimes we have to swallow our pride and move on.

Regarding the second commandment, we've all heard sermons about loving our neighbor as ourselves. This may be part of the greatest commandment but it's also one of the most difficult. There is one thing Jesus said in his comments about this command that I think is extremely practical and useful: Jesus said, "pray for those who persecute you." Some years ago someone hurt our family very badly. Whenever I thought about that person, I could feel my blood pressure go up and anger raging inside of me. One day when I was feeling very angry, these words of Jesus came to me and once they did, whenever I thought of that person, I said a little prayer for the individual. It got rid of all my anger and bitterness. I must confess that doesn't make me perfect. If that person showed up at the rectory wanting to borrow a few hundred dollars, I don't know if I would give it to them (if I had it) – I'm not that far along the road to holiness, but at least my heart is free of anger. There is a lot of benefit in forgiving. Now, when someone tells me that someone is driving them crazy or they are having difficulty forgiving, I say to them, "Jesus says pray for those who persecute you." It will bring you a lot of peace and might even surprise you by helping the other person show more kindness. Amen.

8th Sunday in Ordinary Time
February 27, 2011

INTRODUCTION – (Isaiah 49:14-15; 1 Corinthians 4:1-5; Matthew 6:24-34) The Jews certainly thought God had forgotten them after 50 years of exile in Babylon. But God tells them he hasn't forgotten. The prophet records what God spoke: "Comfort, give comfort to my people, says your God. Speak tenderly to Jerusalem and say to her that her service is at an end, (i.e. the exile is over), her guilt is expiated." (Isaiah 40:1-2) God goes on to tell his people he has written their name on the palm of his hand – an image expressing his continual remembrance of his people. Our very short first reading today is one of the most tender expressions in the Old Testament of God's love for God's people.

HOMILY – Murphy and his buddies were out playing cards one evening and Murphy was soon down $500. After he lost an additional $500 in the next hand, he grabbed his chest and fell over dead. His buddies didn't know what to do, but they knew they had to tell his wife. Sullivan was chosen to tell Murphy's wife. The other guys told him he had to be very gentle, not to shock her and to break it to her easily. He assured them he would be the essence of tactfulness. So he went to the house, knocked on the door and when Mrs. Murphy answered he told her, "Your husband just lost $1000 in a poker game and he is afraid to come home." She replied, "Tell him to drop dead." Sullivan said, "I'll be sure and do that Mrs. Murphy."

Jesus reminds us today in the gospel that we are not in control of that moment when we have to leave this world. Modern medicine may give us a little more time, but we can't avoid the inevitable. He asks us: "Can any of you by worrying add a single moment to your life-span?"

As we continue listening to the Sermon on the Mount, Jesus reminds us that entering the kingdom of heaven is more important than everything else in our lives. In a variety of ways this theme runs all through the Sermon on the Mount. In each part of the Sermon, Jesus tells us something we need to know in order to enter into the heavenly kingdom. Today's passage focuses on our everyday needs and worries.

The people Jesus was speaking to had more basic needs and worries than most of us have. Most of them were just trying to survive. Many people are just trying to survive today too, but most of us have our basic material needs met and so we worry about other things like safety and security, our loved ones, politics, health, the price of gas, whether I should get a new cell phone, worrying whether my nose is too big, keeping up with the Jones', etc. As important as some of our concerns are, God's kingdom is more important. Jesus tells us, "Put God first and have more trust in God."

We must not distort his message like the boy who wrote home from college: "Dear Mom and Dad, today's gospel reading was all about not worrying over things like food and clothing because God is going to give them to us anyway, and it takes our minds away from what really matters. That gave me a whole new perspective. From now on, I'm not going to worry about getting good grades, finding a job, etc. God knows that I need them and God will come through. Your loving son. P.S. In case God is slow getting around to me, I need $800. (from *Preaching Resource,* CelebrationPublications.org, Feb 27, 2011, pg 4)

God expects us to use our brains to deal with life and to provide for ourselves. There is a line in George Bernard Shaw's play Joan of Arc. Joan was discussing with her general whether she should go into battle with an army that vastly outnumbered her own. She said God would help her win. Her general told her, "God is no man's daily drudgery." The general as it turned out was right. Joan lost the battle. God is not going to do for us what we should do for ourselves. He's not going to do our laundry, pay our bills, cut our grass or plant our gardens. We have to do for ourselves what God gave us the power to do.

There are those times when we are not in control. That's when we must trust in God's love and care. If we don't trust, we can worry ourselves to death, but Jesus doesn't want us to do that. There is a line from St. Paul that is very helpful to me. He tells us, "for those who love God, all things work out for the best." (Rom 8:28) Believing that brings me a lot of peace. Amen.

9th Sunday in Ordinary Time
March 6, 2011

INTRODUCTION – (Deut. 11:18, 26-28; Rom. 3:21-25; Mt. 7:21-27) When God's people were oppressed and enslaved in Egypt, Moses brought them out of Egypt and led them to freedom and began to take them to the Promised Land. However, when they arrived, the people rebelled. They were afraid to enter the Land, and wouldn't trust that God would protect them from the inhabitants of the Land, so God let them have their way. Consequently, they lived like nomads in the Sinai desert for many years until a new and more courageous generation had grown up. When that next generation had matured, and all those who rebelled against God and Moses had died, Moses again began to lead God's people toward the Promised Land. This new generation was ready to go. When they reached the Jordan River opposite

Jericho, Moses knew his job was finished and it was time for him to die. So he sought to leave God's people with some last words of wisdom before they would enter the Land. That is the setting for the entire book of Deuteronomy (a word that means "second law.") Moses reminds God's people of everything God demands of them. In today's passage Moses assures them that if they are faithful to God's word, it will be a source of great blessings for them. To ignore God's word will bring great suffering to God's people. The choice is theirs.

HOMILY – One Sunday as the pastor was giving his homily, he heard two girls in the back giggling and disturbing people. He interrupted his homily and announced sternly, "There are two of you here who have not heard one word I've said." That quieted them down. When the service was over, he went to greet the people at the front door. Three adults apologized for going to sleep in church, promising it would never happen again. (from *Reader's Digest, Laughter, the Best Medicine,* pg 61)

That's what Moses had to say to God's people before he was to die. That's what Jesus had to say to his listeners as he ended the Sermon on the Mount. Listen to what I have to say. It is listening not just with our ears, but also with our heart and soul and mind and strength.

This is the fifth week now we have heard a part of the Sermon on the Mount. We haven't heard it all. On Wednesday of this week, we will hear more from Jesus' Sermon regarding three traditional practices that have helped people for centuries to grow in holiness: prayer, fasting and almsgiving. These are subjects that fit perfectly with the theme of Ash Wednesday. Today, however, we hear the conclusion of Jesus' Sermon; an appropriate way to conclude all he had said. Jesus laid before us what we must do to enter the kingdom of heaven, and he ends by telling us it's up to us whether we will make that choice.

Did you happen to notice how the Sermon has pretty much one focus, it is trying to show us the way to the kingdom of heaven. Remember how the Sermon on the Mount begins? The opening sentence is: "Blessed are the poor in spirit, for theirs is the kingdom of heaven." Jesus seems to tell us we are made for the kingdom for we are the salt of the earth and the light of the world. BUT our holiness must surpass that of the scribes and the Pharisees (those who were thought to be the holiest people of all among God's people). If we do not surpass them in holiness, we will not enter into the kingdom of heaven. Jesus followed this up with specific examples of what he meant. After teaching us to pray for the kingdom (Thy kingdom come), then we heard him tell us not to be anxious about our daily needs. We are to seek first the kingdom of God and his righteousness and all these things will be given us besides.

As Jesus finishes his Sermon, he tells us our religion cannot be superficial, it's not just a matter of using the right words or even working great miracles in his name: "Not everyone who says 'Lord, Lord' will enter the kingdom of heaven, but only the one who DOES the will of my Father in Heaven." The kingdom of heaven is all about making Jesus the foundation of our lives.

Jesus' final image is so clear. He pictures us all as builders, and indeed we are. Each day of our lives is like another stone that we put into place as we build our lives. Some build fabulous mansions, some build simple but comfortable homes. God gives us all the supplies we really need. Some don't use all the materials they are given. However, the issue is the foundation. Is it on something solid? If it's not Jesus, it will not be solid enough to withstand the stresses and problems of life. The kingdom of heaven is built on our faith in Jesus, a faith that is not just a matter of saying we believe in him, but is a matter of doing what he told us to do. In John's gospel there is no doubt what building our life on him means when he tells us, "If you love me you will keep my commandments." (John 14:15)

The choice is ours. The kingdom of heaven is not an entitlement. There are numerous parables that tell us that, just as Jesus' Sermon on the Mount tells us that. Years ago I spoke to a mother and young daughter who were seldom at Sunday Mass. I asked why I didn't see them very frequently. The mother told me her daughter was involved in sports and often events were on Sundays. As I tried to tell her how important their religion should be to them, the mother told me: "But Father, you don't understand: sports is her life." We can build our lives on all kinds of things, money, career, pleasure, sports, food, etc. All these things have a place in our lives, but they will eventually fail us if we make them our main support. They are like the sand that fails us in the end. We need to take Jesus as our rock and our foundation. Amen.

1st Sunday in Lent
March 13, 2011

INTRODUCTION – (Genesis 2:7-9 & 3:1-7; Romans 5:12-19; Matthew 4:1-11) Today's first reading tells us the story of the creation of our first parents, their temptation and their fall from grace. The story is more theological than it is historical. It tells us God created the human race to be happy and to share in his grace and friendship. This is indicated by the Garden of Eden. Although all that God made was very good, we know bad things happen in the world, in nature and in the way we deal with one another. This story presents one explanation for the problem of evil in the world, a problem that St. Paul attempts to explain in today's second reading. In these passages we are told that evil finds its source in our decision to give in to temptation, in our attempt to make our own rules and to use our free will to say "no" to God. In the gospel, Jesus, who has come to save us from evil, has shown us how to resist temptation.

HOMILY – A woman was shopping for a new dress and found the most stunning creation she had ever seen. But it was expensive: $750. She knew she couldn't afford it, but she had to at least see how she looked in it. So she tried it on and it made her look beautiful. She knew someone else would see it and buy it before she could ever save up for it and she knew she just had to have it. So she bought it. That evening as she showed her husband how beautiful it was and how beautiful she looked with it on, he asked the inevitable question: "how much did it cost?" When she told him he had a fit. She explained the temptation was more than she could resist. He told her when she is tempted she needs to tell the devil: "get behind me, Satan." She pleaded "that's what I did, and the devil told me it looks fantastic from the back too."

Temptations always attract us to something that looks good, even when we know it will not be good for us in the long run – that is the nature of a temptation. And we are all tempted, even Jesus who was perfect, for he was also human like us in every way except sin. In the temptation about the stones into bread, he was being tempted to use his miraculous powers for his own comfort and convenience. He never did, however. He used his miraculous powers to help others. In the other two temptations, he was being tempted to use his special connection with God to gain a following or to create a kingdom according to the standards of this world. He knew, however, that his kingdom would not be of this world and his place in God's kingdom would be to serve and not to be served. He also knew how much would be demanded of him in order to fulfill his role as messiah and savior. He did not cheat, cut corners or waver in any way.

We use the word temptation often in innocent ways. For example, we might say "that piece of pie is very tempting." In most cases this would not be a temptation to sin. There are those times when we know that if we give in to certain temptations we are following the example of our first parents who thought they were smarter than God and that they could find even greater happiness than God had given them if they did their own thing. It was a sin of disobedience and a sin of failing to trust God's love and wisdom.

The story of Jesus temptation in the desert is put before us at the beginning of Lent to encourage us to follow Jesus' example, to set aside time for prayer and self-sacrifice so we can have the strength to overpower the temptations that come to all of us. These two, prayer and self-sacrifice are two of the traditional practices that lead us to holiness. Self-sacrifice is usually represented as fasting from food, and that probably wouldn't hurt most of us to occasionally cut back somewhat on what we eat. But self-sacrifice does not necessarily have to deal with food; it could be fasting from TV, or nasty comments toward others, or smoking, or the internet or whatever it is that might keep our feet stuck in the mud instead of lifting our minds and hearts more toward love of God and love of others.

A third practice that is traditionally recommended to help lead us to holiness is almsgiving, that is, giving to charity. There is no end of possibilities in this area. We all are aware of the great disaster Japan is experiencing right now. The Archbishop asked all churches to provide an opportunity to help Japan in this emergency and so extra envelopes are in the pews for this purpose. All donations will go to Catholic Relief Services which assists suffering people all over the world and which will certainly be used to help in Japan.

Before the tragedy in Japan, I had my homily written and there was another topic I needed to bring up. Every year around this time we have a special Archdiocesan Collection – formerly misnamed the Archbishop's Annual Fund Drive (since the Archbishop never got any part of it) and which is now appropriately called the Catholic Ministries Appeal. I needed to talk about it today because appeal letters are being sent out this Wednesday from the Archbishop. If you don't get it by the end of this week, you should certainly get it before the end of the month. Your help is needed for the support of major ministries in our Archdiocese. To be brief, I want to mention just three of the major ones: 1) the education of priests, deacons and lay pastoral ministers at the Athenaeum, and if we get more vocations which the Archbishop is trying to do, support for the Athenaeum will be greatly needed; 2) Catholic Charities and Catholic Social Services which provides many services and basic needs to the poor, and 3) the support of retired diocesan priests. This collection helps support Fr. Lammeier in his retirement and someday, if I ever retire, although I'm not in a hurry to, I hope to receive some retirement support from this collection too. This collection takes the place of a pension for priests and the demand in this area keeps increasing because priests, like the rest of society, are living longer. Just those few areas of need I have mentioned take 80 percent of your donation. The other 20 percent will go for chaplains for hospitals and prisons and for St. Rita's School for the Deaf. Nothing is used for Archdiocesan administration. All these worthwhile causes are related to ministries that would be beyond the capability of any single parish to maintain. We do need some substantial gifts to make our goal. I am proud of St. Boniface. Our parish has met our goal every year for the past 19 years that I've been here. So I am very hopeful we will do it again. Our parish goal is $15,937 which is $163 less than last year. Again this year I suggest that if everyone who could afford it, would pledge or donate $100, we would make our goal. However, whatever you can give will be greatly appreciated, even if it's $5 or $10. When you receive Archbishop Schnurr's letter, there will be a pledge card and donation envelope with it. You may send it in to the Archdiocese or to St. Boniface or save yourself 44 cents and bring it with you to church and put it in the collection basket. I hope everyone is tempted to be generous. Thank you.

2nd Sunday in Lent
March 20, 2011

INTRODUCTION – (Genesis 12:1-4; 2 Timothy 1:8b-10; Matthew 17:1-9) Our first reading takes us back almost 4000 years to Abraham. His name was Abram before God gave him a vocation and a new name. Abram came from an ancient civilization known as Sumer, a settlement near modern day Kuwait. He and his family migrated to the northern part of Syria, near Turkey. After a lengthy stay there, he heard God's call to leave his kinfolk behind and move to the land of Canaan – modern day Israel. He left behind a prosperous commercial area to settle in a land that was still relatively primitive and undeveloped. Abraham made this long and difficult journey at the tender age of 75 along with his wife, Sarah, who was 10 years younger.

God was telling them, not only to pack up and move to an unknown territory, but to start a family there as well! It was a pure act of faith on the part of Abraham to follow God's call and to believe in the blessings God kept promising him, promises we hear in today's first reading. In the gospel, we have Matthew's account of the Transfiguration, which was a promise to Jesus' disciples and which is a promise to us of great blessings God has in store for us.

HOMILY – Several years ago the pope came to the United States. As he was being driven from the airport, he was admiring the limo he was riding in. He was so impressed with what a nice car it was that he asked the driver whether he could drive it. How could the driver say "no" to the pope, so he traded places with the pope. The pope was having such fun driving, that before he knew it he was seriously exceeding the speed limit, weaving in and out of traffic and cutting off other drivers. Of course, a policeman spotted him and ran him down. As the policeman walked toward the car, he noticed the man in the back seat but he was really shocked when he saw who was driving. He walked back to his squad car and radioed the police chief. He said "I don't know what to do. I just flagged down a really important person." The chief said "well give him a ticket." The officer said, "you don't understand. He's really important." The chief said "well who is it, a Senator, the governor, the president?" The officer said, "I don't know who he is, but whoever he is, he's got the pope as his chauffer."

Today we hear about Jesus whose importance far outweighs anyone who ever lived. St. Matthew tells us today of Jesus' transfiguration. The event is recorded four times in the New Testament. In all three of the gospels, the transfiguration is preceded by Peter's confession of

Jesus as Messiah. Jesus had asked the disciples, "Who do people say that I am?" He then asked, "Who do you say that I am?" In Mark and Luke, Peter answered, "you are the Messiah." In Matthew, Peter adds "... the Son of the Living God." After this wonderful profession of faith, Jesus began to teach the apostles that he would suffer, be put to death and on the third day be raised. That's when Peter got in trouble with Jesus. He told Jesus none of that would happen to him. No one at that time, no teacher or writing, connected the two, for the messiah was to be a powerful leader who would victoriously conquer all the enemies of the Jewish people and establish forever a kingdom of peace and justice under God's rule.

I think those who chose the reading for the transfiguration left out three very important words in today's gospel. The gospel should begin, "After six days" or "six days later" (Luke tells us "eight days" but you get the idea). How often do we see this in the gospels when two events are linked together in this way. Most of the time, Jesus' teachings and miracles are strung together like "pearls on a string" as one scholar described it, without much attention to sequence. An event that took place late in Jesus' ministry might be recounted as having taken place early in his ministry by another of the gospel writers. The cleansing of the Temple would be a prime example. But here, the transfiguration is definitely connected with the question of who Jesus is and the sufferings he would have to face. In Fr. Bruce Vwater's marvelous book (which I use so much that it's practically falling apart), a book entitled: *The Four Gospels*, Fr. Vwater tells us "Peter's confession and its sequel (i.e. the passion) ... form a unit with the transfiguration to set forth in all its fullness what the ... gospels want to say of the historical Jesus as the Christ." The transfiguration is a visible manifestation of who Jesus is and where his sufferings would lead. Lest there be any doubt about the matter, God the Father spoke up to make things clear: "This is my beloved Son, with whom I am well pleased."

How does all that apply to us? It gives us hope in our own times of suffering. Suffering and death will not have the last word in the lives of those who follow Jesus for just as Jesus could predict that he would be raised, he promises us a share in his glory and in his kingdom: "For this is the will of my Father, that everyone who sees the Son and believes in him may have eternal life, and I shall raise him on the last day." (John 6:40)

It is a promise, an assurance, a message to give us hope through difficult times. The apostles wanted to stay on the mountain. It was so wonderful experiencing God's glory as it was displaying itself in Jesus. Jesus' work was ahead of him, so this event was only a preview. Jesus had to leave the mountain and come back down to earth, back to the day-to-day ministry to God's people and dealing with the suffering he knew he would have to face, and they would have to do the same. Until they (and we) enter into eternal glory with Jesus, God the Father gives a word of guidance and direction to all who would follow his Son: "Listen to him." It only stands to reason that we won't do a very good job of following if we don't listen. Amen.

3rd Sunday in Lent
March 27, 2011

INTRODUCTION – (Exodus 17:3-7; Romans 5:1-2.5-8; John 4:5-42) In our first reading, we hear of an event that takes place as Moses is leading God's people through the desert to the Promised Land. It was probably two or three months since they left Egypt. Twice the

Bible tells us God had provided, in a marvelous way, food and water for them. They needed water again. It sounds as if even Moses doesn't know what to do next to get the people the water they need for themselves, their children and their livestock. God, of course, took care of them. The reading prepares us for the gospel when we hear Jesus offer "living water" to a woman he meets in Samaria as he is traveling south toward Jerusalem. She misunderstands the term "living water" until Jesus reveals to her that it is something that Jesus can give that would sustain her throughout this life's journey and into eternal life. He offers this living water to us today as we meet him in faith and prayer.

HOMILY – A little child came home one day from religion class and his mother asked him what he learned. He answered, "all about Moses; how God sent Moses behind enemy lines to rescue God's people who were slaves in Egypt. The teacher told how Moses led them as far as the Red Sea. Then he had his engineers build a pontoon bridge so all the people could cross the Sea. Then he dynamited the bridge after they crossed so the Egyptians couldn't catch up with them. And then all God's people traveled safely through a desert to the Promised Land." His mother said, "Now, Brad, is that what the teacher really taught you?" Brad answered, "Well, no mom, but if I told you the way she really told us, you would never believe it."

It does take a lot of faith to believe in all the miracles mentioned in the Bible. Today we hear about another one as God miraculously provides water from a rock for his people during their desert journey. Today, in his marvelous storytelling style, John tells us about Jesus who desires to offer all who would believe in him living water, a miracle infinitely more wondrous than the fabled fountain of youth. Jesus very cleverly introduces the idea by asking for a drink. The Samaritan woman was shocked – not only because Jews and Samaritans hated one another and had nothing to do with one another, but also because in that culture men never spoke with women in public, least of all one who was a stranger. By offering living water, Jesus was deliberately vague, offering something she would see as a great convenience, without having any idea how precious a gift it is he offers. Notice how Jesus controls the conversation and he keeps directing her to faith in himself. When he brings up something personal about her, her intimate life with a man to whom she is not married, then it gets really spooky for her. She quickly changes the subject, but he persists in fascinating her – so much so that she becomes fascinated enough to spread the word to her neighbors about this unique person she had met.

Living water is not the only image or symbol Jesus uses to reveal who he is and the eternal life he came to bring us; he refers to himself as the bread of life, the light of the world, the good shepherd, the lamb of God, the vine of which we are the branches, the resurrection and the life, just to name a few of the other images Jesus uses. The important message I get from today's reading is that the more we engage with Jesus in reflection and prayer, even in spite of distractions, the more he seeks to lead us into a deeper relationship with himself and with the Father. Amen.

4th Sunday of Lent
March 2, 2008

INTRODUCTION – (1 Samuel 16:1b, 6-7, 10-13a, Ephesians 5:8-14, John 9:1-41) Sight is a wonderful gift, but what we see with our mind and heart is even of greater value. God helps us to see clearly. We have examples of that inner vision in all of today's readings. Our first reading takes us back 1000 years before Christ when the prophet Samuel had to choose a king from among the sons of Jesse of Bethlehem. They all had the dignity and physical characteristics of potentially good leaders, but God knew who would make the best king. Paul tells us we have been enlightened by Christ and in the gospel we hear how a man born blind not only had his eyes opened by Christ but his heart, whereas those who claimed to be able to see were blinded by arrogance.

HOMILY – Two weeks ago, I appealed to all of our parishioners for their support of the Catholic Ministries Appeal. It is going well. We are about $2500 short of our $15,000 goal. I am most grateful to all who have responded. There has been one item that a few people have been confused about. In past years, at this time of the year, we have had the Archdiocesan Fund Drive. Some are wondering if another appeal is coming next. The answer is: No!

I wanted to make another appeal to you today, not for money, but for your involvement at Mass. You might have noticed that last week and this week we've been singing some hymns you might not have heard for years, such as All the Earth Proclaim the Lord; Yes, I Shall Arise; My Soul is Longing for Your Peace. Next week you will hear them again. I have asked Don to schedule these pieces in testimony to their composer: Fr. Lucien Deiss. Fr. Deiss died about five months ago and he was a pioneer in composing liturgical music 45 years ago as the language of the Mass was going from Latin to English. He was also a scholar in Sacred Scripture and Patristics (that is the study of the early Fathers of the Church). I had the opportunity to attend a workshop by him when I was first ordained and I was deeply impressed. Much of his music is no longer in use today (except for Keep in Mind) but I thought his passing should not go unnoticed.

I thought I would take this occasion as we remember him, to stress the importance of music at Mass. I've told you my story about when I was a child, whenever we had singing practice, the good sisters in school encouraged me to listen. They said that way I would learn to sing if I listened to the others. It wasn't until I was 20 or 21 that our choir director in the seminary called me aside after chant practice and offered to give me individual lessons in singing. I think it helped. The point I'm trying to make is that if you think you can't sing, you'll never learn how if you don't try. Sometimes people say to me I don't know that hymn we had today. But if a person doesn't try to sing it they'll never know it. I don't know if people have ever noticed but the hymns we choose try to correspond to the liturgical season and the theme of the readings. Hopefully, if a hymn is unfamiliar, over the course of time we will become more comfortable with it. We'll never learn any new ones any other way. I know that musical tastes vary. Some people like the more traditional ones and others like the more modern ones, some people like the slow, prayerful ones and some like those with a fast, lively beat. Don tries to vary them, I know. The important thing is that they represent quality music. But sometimes good music is not always appreciated right away. While I was on vacation, I watched a movie on the life of Cole Porter. There was a comment he made in the movie that struck me. He said "I often get paid much less for a really good piece of music than I get paid for that that's not very good." As with many other things in life, popularity does not represent quality and vice-versa. And the music we use should be good quality.

When everyone sings, the prayer is uplifting and energizing. Singing gets a person more involved and engaged in the Mass. And the time seems to go by quickly. I noticed when I can't sing (like if I have a sore throat), the time goes much more slowly. Maybe this is what St. Augustine meant when he said: "he who sings, prays twice." We put more of ourselves into the prayer when we sing. I have two suggestions: if people would move up further in church, they could support one another with their singing and this would give more a sense of community. The other suggestion is to open your hymn book to the hymn and if you can't sing it or don't feel comfortable even trying, just read the words that are being sung, for they are a prayer. That's all I'll say. The more involved you are in the Mass, the more a blessing it will be for you. Amen.

5th Sunday of Lent
March 9, 2008

HOMILY – (Ezekiel 37:12-14, Romans 8:8-11, John 11:1-45) Bertrand Russell said: success is getting what you want; happiness is wanting what you get. I don't think many of us wanted all this snow, but what Bertrand Russell said implies that we do our best to adjust to the ups and downs of life. Thank God we have our faith to help us along the way and to give us hope.

The greatest hope we have is that life will never end.

Today's gospels is one of my very favorite ones, because it was while I was visiting the tomb of Lazarus in Bethany that I had an overwhelming experience of the divine presence of Jesus.

Jesus said to Martha: "I am the resurrection and the life; whoever believes in me, even if he dies, will live, and everyone who lives and believes in me will never die." Who could make such a statement: "everyone who lives and believes in me will never die?" They would either have to be someone so unique and special, the likes of which this world has never known, or they would have to be someone severely delusional. From everything else we know about Jesus, he was totally sane and in touch with reality. More than that he was someone with special wisdom and special powers. He did not just ask for Martha's faith, "do you believe this?" but he did more, he showed he had power even over death itself. Who else has the power to make the tombs empty? The Lord asks us today as he asked Martha: "Do you believe this?" "Do you believe that everyone who lives and believes in me will never die?" What a comfort this is when we lose a loved one whom we know has lived and died in God's grace.

But Jesus' words are not limited to the experience of death. We all experience many losses in life, little deaths, things that we have to grieve for. It could be our health, our job, our security or the loss of something that meant a lot to us. We have to trust somehow that even in these sufferings God can bring life out of death. This is what is meant by the Easter mystery, or the Paschal mystery that we are preparing to celebrate. As St. Paul tells us: "We know that all things work for good for those who love God." Rom 8:28.

This is the hope that I live by and that gives new life to all of us. Amen.

Passion Sunday
April 17, 2011

HOMILY – Jesus came as a savior. He came to heal people, to free them from the powers of evil, to teach that we must love one another and care for one another; he came to show us the way to freedom from fear, freedom from sin that destroys us, the way to true peace and happiness. He came into Jerusalem to shouts of "Hosanna" which in Hebrew means, "Save us, we pray." Even though it would cost him his life, he would not give up his mission or run away from it.

He did not want to see people have to suffer and yet ... and yet he tells us "whoever does not carry his own cross and come after me cannot be my disciple." (Lk. 14:27; cf also Mk. 8:34, Mt. 10:38 & 16:24 and Lk. 9:23). We find this challenging statement several times in the gospels. It's not what we would prefer to hear. I would prefer to hear Jesus say something like he says in John's gospel: "If you ask anything of me in my name, I will do it." (Jn. 14:14) We know that doesn't always happen ... at least not in this life.

Various verbs are used to express this thought "take up your cross," such as, "carry your own cross" or "make it your own" or "endure it." One author I was reading lately (*Swimming in the Sun* by Albert Haase OFM) used the word "embrace it." "Embracing your cross" has the connotation of loving it. When I came across that word "embrace," it was like a shock. I could see enduring it or suffering it, but embracing it??? The more I thought about it, the more I realized it's the attitude the saints had when they had to deal with their crosses. I'm not advocating looking for suffering like a masochist. If we have problems, we try to solve them. If we are sick we see a doctor; that is the rational thing to do. We all deal with suffering that is unavoidable and inescapable. That's where Jesus was in his ministry. If he were to be faithful to his mission, he would pay a great price. That's what he had to do to be true to himself and his Father. For Jesus, for the saints, and for all of us (as I came to see) surrender, acceptance and hope are the way to prevent any cross from destroying us. I've seen it happen many times. When a person finally accepts what he or she knows they cannot change, and even embrace it knowing it will bring them closer to God, I've seen them experience a deep peace. That is the message in the cross, that is the message in the resurrection. God will not let us down. For those who love him, everything works out for the best. Amen.

Holy Thursday
April 21, 2011

HOMILY – We have heard in our readings about the first Holy Thursday. The first reading describes the Jewish feast of Passover which Jesus and his disciples were celebrating. This ancient remembrance of God's saving love had been observed for over 1000 years before the time of Christ. St. Paul tells us in the second reading how Jesus originated a new way for God's people to celebrate God's saving love in the Eucharist. This is the earliest document of the institution of the Eucharist that we have. Paul's letter was written about the year 56 or 57. That's about a dozen or so years before the first gospel, the gospel of Mark, was written. Then in this evening's gospel from John we are told how Jesus demonstrated for his disciples, and for all who would be his disciples, the great lesson of love that he constantly taught. It was a demonstration of love and service that he would subsequently show in giving us the Eucharist and in giving his life on the cross.

This was the last meal Jesus would have with his disciples. He had enjoyed many meals with them since he had first called them to follow him. As they gathered for the last time, we wonder what must have been in his mind and heart? He knew what he would soon have to face and what his disciples would soon have to face. He knew he had many enemies because of his teachings. He knew that as a prophet, he would face the same destiny that most of the prophets suffered including his own cousin, John the Baptist. Although they remained in a state of denial whenever he tried to tell them, he had even warned his apostles of what would happen,

The best indication of what was in Jesus' mind and heart at the last supper is revealed to us by what he said and did that night. In the preliminary part of the Passover meal, Jesus told his disciples how much he desired to share that meal with them. He would not eat it again until it is fulfilled in the kingdom of God. Then he blessed either the first or second cup of wine (there were always four servings of wine at Passover) and he told them I will not drink of the fruit of the vine until the kingdom of God comes. (Lk 22:16-17) These words of blessing tell us Jesus saw his death as the means by which God's kingdom would begin – when God would save his people from the evils of the present age. These words also tell us that this last meal was also a pledge that God would vindicate Jesus even beyond death and bring him and his followers into God's eternal kingdom.

Sometime, during the meal, Jesus washed his disciples feet and then interpreted what he had done: "if I, the master and teacher, have washed your feet, you ought to wash one another's feet." Sometime during the meal he also revealed that one of them was going to betray him. Judas was identified but not to the group. Then Judas left the upper room.

The meal itself started with the breaking of the bread. In the typical Passover liturgy, the head of the house took the bread for distribution as a symbol of how he provided for his own. Jesus now provided, not bread, but himself for his own. To his dying breath, Jesus continued to feed his disciples. He took bread, said the blessing, broke it, and gave it to them saying, "This is my body which will be given for you." The word "body" does not mean a mere body, but one's entire life, the whole human being.

Most likely it was the fourth cup, the cup of blessing after the meal, that Jesus told them to share for he identified that cup as "the new covenant in my blood which will be shed for you." The cup is a reference to the covenant of Sinai which united the partners to the covenant, God and God's people, into one. Jesus' blood would unite us in a life-giving relationship with himself, for blood was seen by the Jews to somehow contain life. And in that is salvation – sharing in Christ's divine life. That Jesus had them share the same cup would have been unusual for normally each person had their own cup to drink out of. It showed that in this cup they might all remain united with him.

Jesus died as he had lived: He came to serve, not to be served. His death was for us. His body is for us: "This is my body that is for you," we hear him say in Paul's letter. The fact that he gives his body for us implies the salvific nature of his death. Through our union with him, he shares his divine life with us, a life that someday we will enjoy in eternal glory. If a person did not understand all of this, St. John made it clear in the sixth chapter of his gospel where Jesus says: "unless you eat the flesh of the Son of Man and drink his blood, you have no life in you. Whoever eats my flesh and drinks my blood has eternal life and I will raise him on the last day." (Jn. 6:55-56)

As Jesus has given his life for others, in ministry, in service and in death, so too must his disciples give their lives in service to others. The Eucharist and the washing of feet give us the same message. In serving us, Christ has given us a model, that we should serve one another. Amen.

Good Friday
April 2, 2010

HOMILY – (Is 52:13-53:12; Heb 4:14-16, 5:7-9; John 18:1-19:42) Every day we gather around this altar to celebrate the Eucharist. In the Eucharist God's love is shown to us through Jesus Christ who gave his life for us on the cross. So he can share his life with us now, he continues to give us his body and blood. The gift of his life involved immense suffering on his part. Our gospels do not dwell long on his sufferings. They didn't need to because the people who lived at the time the gospels were written knew what crucifixion involved. It was one of the most agonizing forms of execution that human beings had ever concocted. On this one day of the year, out of respect for what Jesus went through, we do not celebrate the Eucharist as we do every other day. Instead we have a rather extended service of reflection, intercessions, and Communion.

Rather than focusing on the physical sufferings of Jesus, I would like to reflect on the mystery of suffering itself. The book of Genesis attributes suffering to sin. The first man and woman God created lost the happiness God had intended for them because of their disobedience to God. The whole first part of the Old Testament, Deuteronomy, Judges, Samuel and Kings and many of the prophets reflects this notion of suffering – that it is caused by disobedience to God. There is some truth in that notion, but it is not the whole story as the Book of Job tells us. Without telling us why good people suffer, the Book of Job took issue with the old theology on suffering. Sometime about 500 years before Christ, the prophet Isaiah gave us a new way of thinking about suffering – that it can have a positive purpose – that one person's suffering can bring blessings to another. We heard it clearly expressed in today's first reading from a passage in Isaiah known as the 4th Servant Song. I would like to repeat some phrases from our first reading; they are so powerful. God's Servant, Isaiah says, "was spurned and avoided by people, a man of suffering, accustomed to infirmity...Yet it was our infirmities that he bore, our sufferings that he endured...he was pierced for our offenses, crushed for our sins; upon him was the chastisement that makes us whole, by his stripes we were healed...though he had done no wrong nor spoken any falsehood, the Lord was pleased to crush him in infirmity... he shall take away the sins of many and win pardon for their offenses."

It is easy to see in a family how one person's sufferings can benefit another person. For example, how parents make sacrifices for their children, how they have to go through difficult times to support those they love and teach them and discipline them. The sufferings of Jesus, however, were a scandal to his followers. The Messiah was not expected to suffer. We remember when Jesus tried to warn his disciples that he would "suffer greatly and be killed and would rise again." Peter replied, "Heaven forbid, Lord, this will never happen to you." Jesus response to Peter is familiar to all of us: "Get behind me, Satan."

Why did he have to suffer? I have asked myself that

question many times and others have asked me that question many times as well. My current thinking on this is I think he had to suffer because of who he was. He was God's Son who came among a sinful people. He could not be anything other than who he was and, without redemption, we could not be anything other than who we are. He was like a lamb dropped into a tigers' cage. He was from above, we are from this world, his holiness did not fit in with our sinful ways. The only kingdom we could know was the kingdom of this world and his kingdom did not belong to this world. Thus he came to his own and his own received him not. Because he could not be other than who he was and because he was faithful to the purpose for which he came – his purpose being to confront the powers of evil, to heal and to teach us to change our lives and to live in a new way – conflict, confrontation, rejection and suffering were inevitable. Yet his sufferings led to his resurrection and glorification. Jesus has "passed through the heavens," as the Letter to the Hebrews tells us, to take his rightful place at God's right hand. But he has not left us, rather through his Spirit, through prayer and the sacraments and through his love in us he has transformed us and made us sharers in his new life. He has made us into a new creation. "He has become the source of eternal life for all who obey him," the Letter to the Hebrews tells us. Or as Isaiah tells us: "By his stripes we were healed." Amen.

Easter
April 24, 2011

HOMILY – A middle-aged couple, whose last child had recently moved out on her own, were having a conversation right before Easter. The wife said to her husband that with the children grown and away from home, this was their first year they were not going to dye Easter eggs and have an Easter egg hunt. To console her, her husband responded, "That's alright, honey, we can just hide each other's pills."

I'm sure we all remember the hymn, "Were you there when they crucified my Lord." The second verse still echoes in my mind from Good Friday: "Were you there when they nailed him to the tree." Most crosses we see are made of two pieces of nicely trimmed lumber, but I would bet the Romans didn't take the time to trim the bark off many crosses. They probably looked like our own cross; like two stout tree limbs.

I listened to a lecture recently about the meaning of Jesus' death and resurrection, (a lecture given by Professor Bart Ehrman and recorded by The Teaching Company). (cf also: Fitzmeier, *The New Jerome Biblical Commentary*, 82:14) The lecture was very illuminating to me and I would like to share some of its ideas with you. It approached the death and resurrection from the way St. Paul might have approached it. St. Paul, as you know, taught us a lot about the resurrection. Paul was a strict Jew and he at first persecuted the Christians for believing in Jesus as the Messiah. He knew Jewish law and it is written in the law of Deuteronomy: "cursed is everyone who hangs on a tree." (Deut 21:23) This would have meant to Paul that Jesus was a great sinner and that's why he was crucified. But Jesus appeared to Paul one day and called him to task for persecuting his followers. Actually Jesus identified himself with his followers and said, "why are you persecuting me?" Paul would have had to wonder if Christ was cursed by God because he was a terrible sinner, as the law said, then why did God raise him back to life? There was only one possible answer to that question for Paul: rather than being a condemned criminal, cursed to die on a cross,

Jesus must have been a man of exceptional holiness to have been so uniquely blessed by God. As such a holy person, the curse of his death was not due to anything Jesus did to displease God, rather he must have borne that curse for others. Thus Paul says in Galatians: "Christ became a curse for us." (Gal. 3:13) In other words, with a logic that only a Pharisee could appreciate, Jesus took upon himself the curse of the Law, and his death was a sacrifice for the sins of others. Jesus' resurrection became the way to forgiveness of sin and a new life of holiness for those who accept him into their lives. As Paul tells us, God will declare us holy if we believe in the One who raised Jesus our Lord from the dead, "who was handed over for our offenses and was raised up for our justification." (Romans 4:25) To say this in the simplest way possible, Jesus had to die and rise so we could rise with him. Paul's experience of seeing the risen Jesus turned his life around. Paul was one of many who saw the risen Christ, but it was probably not for a year or two after Jesus ascended to the Father.

For a few minutes I want to talk about today's gospel from Matthew. Matthew tells us about two of Jesus' women followers: Mary Magdalene and another Mary. They were one of the first people to see Jesus after the resurrection. They had watched Jesus die and saw where he was buried. They came to Jesus' tomb just as the sun was coming up on Easter Sunday morning. Probably they came to continue grieving. Matthew had already told us that the Jewish leaders asked Pilate to place soldiers at the tomb to keep anyone from stealing Jesus' body and then claiming he had risen. So, since a guard was there, the women probably weren't planning on entering the tomb. By the way, none of the gospels describe Jesus' actually rising for it is an event that is beyond description. All the gospels tell us only of things that happened on Easter Sunday. When Jesus died there was an earthquake. Matthew tells us there was another one when Jesus rose from the dead. Matthew wants us to know that Jesus' death and resurrection are of cosmic importance, shaking the foundations of the world. Then Matthew describes an angel who comes down from heaven and who rolls back the stone and sits upon it. The angel did not roll the stone back so Jesus could come out, but so that people could see in and know that Jesus had risen. The powerful Roman guards are like dead men – so frightened were they in the presence of the angel. Worldly powers are no match for the powers of heaven. The angel tells the women, "do not be afraid," and gives the women instructions to tell the apostles about Jesus' resurrection. It was, as it were, their reward for coming to see the tomb, to be able to announce this good news to the apostles. They get a further reward when Jesus appears to them while they were on their way to announce the good news to the apostles, whom Jesus calls "my brothers." Jesus also tells the women, "do not be afraid," and repeats the instructions they had received from the angel. They approach Jesus, embrace his feet and do him homage. This not only shows that Jesus' body was real, it demonstrates affection for Jesus and reverence for him. Matthew is perhaps giving us a hint of how we might approach our Lord – without fear and with affection and reverence.

We have many opportunities to approach our Lord in this way, through acts of love for others, through spiritual reading, the Scriptures and daily prayer, but there is no way that is superior to the Mass in this regard. When we come to Mass, the risen Christ is truly present in the assembly, in his word and in the sacrament and each Mass is a perfect act of worship to God because every Mass celebrates and reenacts the Easter mystery. As St. Paul tells us: "When we eat this bread and drink this cup, we proclaim the death of the Lord until he comes." Amen.

Second Sunday of Easter
April 30/May 1, 2011

INTRODUCTION – (Acts 2:42-47; 1 Peter 1:3-9; John 20:19-31) In our first reading today, St. Luke gives us a lovely picture of the early Church – how it was like one big happy family where everyone was agreeable with one another and cared about each other. If we read a little further in the Acts of the Apostles, we see this idyllic condition didn't last very long, especially as the Church grew and became more complex. Even if the Church is not as unified as it was then, the basic elements of the community that St. Luke identifies for us still form the Church today. They devoted themselves, St. Luke tells us, (1) to the teachings of the apostles, (2) to the communal life, (3) to the breaking of bread (their term for the Eucharist or the Lord's Supper) and (4) to the prayers. This statement tells us in general that being a member of the Church is more than just a matter of calling ourselves a Catholic or having our name on some Church's roster. Being Catholic involves (1) seeking to grow in our faith, (2) caring about one another, (3) participation in the Eucharist, and (4) taking time to pray. An inactive believer is not a believer at all, or as St. James tells us: "Faith without works is dead." (James 2:17)

HOMILY – I understand this is a true story from Texas. Drummond's Bar in Mt. Vernon Texas decided to expand their facilities. The local Baptist church, which disapproves of drinking alcohol, started a prayer campaign to prevent the bar from expanding. Construction on the bar progressed up until the week before the grand opening when lightning struck and burned the entire bar to the ground. After the bar burned, the church folks started bragging about "the power of prayer." So the bar owner sued the church on the grounds that the church "was ultimately responsible for the demise of his building, either through direct or indirect action or means." In response to the accusation, the church denied all responsibility to the burning of the building. The judge read through the bar owner's charges and the church's response and commented: "I don't know how I'm going to rule on this, but it appears that we have a bar owner who believes in the power of prayer, and an entire Baptist church congregation that now does not. (from the internet)

Our gospel today touches on a number of themes with faith being one of them. Jesus offers his friends his own special peace. He gives them a commission to continue his work ("as the Father has sent me, so I send you"). As a helper in this ministry, he gives them the Holy Spirit, and one of the works of Jesus they would do would be to forgive sins. This passage gave rise to the designation of this Sunday as Divine Mercy Sunday. God's mercy, however, is not limited to this one Sunday. God is ready to forgive us any time we approach him with true sorrow for our sins. Then we have the memorable story of Thomas who missed Jesus' first appearance and refused to believe in Jesus' resurrection until he had concrete proof. Jesus gave it to him the following week. Finally, Jesus proclaims all of us blessed who have not experienced what Thomas and the others experienced: "blessed are those who have not seen and have believed."

What I have chosen to talk about for the rest of this homily may seem to some people as being a strange topic; however, I am sure most of us have at times wished we could see our Lord as Thomas and the others did; maybe even have a conversation with him. We envision this would greatly enhance our faith. I had often thought that if Jesus appeared to more people, maybe more people would believe in him.

A few weeks ago I was reading the book *The Science of the Cross* by Saint Edith Stein, a Jewish nun who was killed in a concentration camp. She was a brilliant philosopher, and in her book she was examining the teachings of St. John of the Cross, a doctor of the Church. The book talks about visions under the general treatise on the topic of faith. I am significantly summarizing their thoughts on this, for St. Edith Stein goes on for several pages talking about this matter. She says faith informs us of things we have never seen nor heard. It is a form of supernatural knowledge, knowledge we cannot acquire in any natural way through our senses or through reason. Faith does not contradict reason, but what it communicates to us cannot be acquired by reason. In this life we cannot grasp what God is. It is only through faith (on our part) and grace (on God's part) that we can make progress in knowing God and in growing in union with God. John of the Cross says simply, "the greater one's faith the closer is one's union with God." In considering visions or apparitions, the book goes on to teach that when they come from God, then God will accomplish whatever he wishes to accomplish through them, but we should never dare to desire such sensory apprehensions because such desires do not help us to live by faith. Desiring signs and visions to base our faith on holds us back from growing in faith and prevents the spirit from soaring to the invisible.

Thomas and the other apostles, of course, had to see our risen Lord for it would be their mission to give witness to the resurrection of Christ (something they would have had to see in order to be credible witnesses). And that's what they did. The Greek word for witnesses is μάρτυρες (martyrs). We don't know if Thomas actually touched our Lord, but we hear how Thomas' vision of Jesus took him beyond what the eyes could see to a greater level of faith when he declares: "My Lord and my God." And the gospel ends with the statement that it is blessed to have believed even though we have not seen. And the next to the last chapter of John's gospel ends by telling us that through this faith we have life in his name, a life that will lead us to someday see God face to face in eternal glory.

Third Sunday of Easter
May 8, 2011

Delivered at the 50th Wedding Anniversary Mass at St. Peter in Chains Cathedral.

I am honored to celebrate with you today. I'm Fr. Joe Robinson, pastor of St. Boniface Church. I am also the dean of the Cathedral Deanery and it was because I am dean that I originally thought that's why I was invited to preside at today's liturgy. But the idea did cross my mind that since I have been ordained for 47 years, maybe I was asked to come because I'm about as old as everyone else here. That way you all would feel more comfortable. Maybe with a little luck and God's blessing, I'll make it to my 50th anniversary in a few years. A 50th anniversary is something worth celebrating and something worth giving thanks for that is what we are doing here today.

I have three little stories you might enjoy (all three are from *Reader's Digest: Laughter, the Best Medicine*, pgs. 154, 163 & 175):

1) A lady was telling her friend that after she and her husband had a huge argument, they ended up not talking to each other. Finally, on the third day, he asked where one of his shirts was. "Oh," she said, "now you are speaking to me." He was confused and asked: "What are you talking about?" "Haven't you noticed I haven't spoken to you for three days?" she asked. "No," he said. "I just thought we were getting along."

2) A lady and her sister in law were discussing how long they've been married. The sister-in-law commented: "you've been married to my brother for 50 years. That's a long time." "A long, long time" she agreed. Then she smiled and said: "you know the strangest idea occurred to me the other day. If I had killed your brother the first time I felt like it, I'd be out of jail by now."

3) A husband and wife were comparing notes one day. She pointed out to him, "I have a higher IQ, did better on my SAT's and made more money than you." "Yeah," he said. "But when you look at the big picture, I'm still way ahead of you." Puzzled she asked: "How do you figure?" "I married better," he replied.

So, in the name of the Church, in the name of the sacredness of the sacrament of marriage, I thank you for your 50 years of dedication and love for each other. I thank you for doing more than just silently getting along and for not killing one another when you felt like it. I hope today that you each feel deep in your heart that you got the better part of the deal when you got married.

Leonard Pitts, whose editorials appear in the Enquirer, wrote one a week ago that was inspired by the marriage of Prince William and Kate Middleton. I am going to steal some of his ideas, ideas that are profound, ideas that will not surprise any of you but are always worth remembering. He said marriage is an act of faith. It is a willingness to make a bet that it's possible to love someone always and forever. As you all know, loving each other always and forever is not just romance. It is as much a function of commitment and work as it is a function of love. The capacity and willingness to make that bet, to put in the required work, to be faithful to a commitment, are slowly disappearing from American life. Fifty years ago 70 percent of all American adults were married. Now it's about 54 percent. As so many marriages end in disaster, for numerous reasons, marriage in this day and age is an act of hope as well as an act of faith. It is an act of defiance against cynicism and pessimism. St. Paul has given us one of the best descriptions there is of love when he tells us it is patient and kind, it is not jealous or snobbish or rude or self-seeking, not prone to anger or holding grudges. There is no limit to its forbearance, its trust, its hope, its power to endure. If people have that kind of love, no wonder Paul can say, "love never fails."

Our gospel today presents us with the picture of Jesus' frightened and frustrated disciples. This wasn't the first time they were frightened or frustrated by our Lord nor was it the last time. The kingdom he came to offer would be much greater than they were capable of imagining. The way into that kingdom would be the cross. Through good times and bad, he never abandoned them even when they deserted him. In our journey through life sometimes things can get pretty discouraging. Things don't always happen the way we think they should and we feel anger, discouragement and sadness. Through good times and bad, our Lord is with us, although we do not always recognize him. He has won victory for us over all those forces that seek to pull us down. He has declared victory even over our ultimate enemy – sin and death. It is that victory that we celebrate especially during this Easter season. All through the year Jesus is with us, teaching us with his word in the Scriptures and nourishing us with the bread of his own flesh and blood as he does today.

Again I congratulate you and thank you for over-coming the challenges and fears and discouragements we all face at times throughout our lives. I congratulate you and thank you for your patience, your many sacrifices, your sensitivity to one another, your care and concern, your enduring love. May you trust in our Lord's presence with you and always experience hope and joy and a love that never fails. Amen.

Fourth Sunday of Easter
May 15, 2011

INTRODUCTION – (Acts 2:14a, 36-41; 1 Peter 2:20b-25; John 10:1-10) Pentecost is the setting for our first reading. After the Holy Spirit came down upon Jesus' first followers, the Apostles left the upper room where they were gathered and started speaking in a variety of languages so that people from all over the Mediterranean world, who were in Jerusalem that day, could understand them in their native language. With all the excitement, others were wondering what was going on and so Peter addressed the crowd. Today's reading is the conclusion of Peter's sermon. He proclaims Jesus is Lord and Christ; i.e., as Lord, Jesus is divine and as Christ, Jesus is the Messiah, the savior of God's people. In the second reading from the first letter of Peter, the saving mission of Jesus is proclaimed, so that we, like lost sheep, could be brought back to God.

HOMILY – A young man was trying to get a job with the circus, any job at all. The manager decided to give him a chance to be assistant lion tamer and took him to the lion's cage. The head lion tamer was a beautiful young lady who was just about to rehearse her act. She stepped into the cage, removed her cape with a flourish, displaying a gorgeous costume and she spoke a command to the lion. Obediently the lion crept towards her and then rolled over twice before it sat on its hind legs to beg for a treat. "Well," the manager said to the young man, "do you think you can learn to do that?" "I'm sure I could," he replied, "but first you'll have to get that lion out of there." From *Reader's Digest, Laughter, the Best Medicine*, pg 67)

Just as the lion recognized the voice of its trainer, Jesus tells us in today's gospel the sheep recognize the voice of their shepherd. Sheep will not follow a stranger because they do not recognize the voice of a stranger. There is an irony here. John tells us the Pharisees did not realize what Jesus was trying to tell them for they never accepted Jesus as their shepherd. They didn't realize he was talking about them. In the ancient Near East, the title of shepherd was applied both to kings and to gods. The prophet Ezekiel, 500 years before Christ, condemned the rulers of Israel because they were leading God's people astray and he promised the people God Himself would come to lead his people to justice and holiness. In today's parable, the first point Jesus makes is to tell the Pharisees and Sadducees they were about to lose their job of shepherding God's people for they did not enter by the gate. The gate represents Jesus, and as the gate is the only way into the sheepfold, Jesus is the only one who can bring us to God. The second point he makes is that his sheep hear his voice. We are truly his followers only if we listen to him. There are ways he gave us by which we can hear his voice: prayer and Scripture and in the voices of those who speak his truth. One who speaks the truth may be a person we like as well as a person we dislike; one who speaks the truth may be a wise friend, a parent, a neighbor, a saint like Mother Theresa, or someone who may not be a saint at all but whose words are true. Somehow when we are in the habit of listening for Jesus' voice through prayer and Scripture, we come to recognize Jesus' words when they come to us through other sources. One such source through which our Shepherd speaks is the hierarchy of the Church (pope, bishops, priests and deacons). As we know, the hierarchy is human and as such has its weaknesses and sins. We who are ordained have to go to confession just like everyone else, but in spite of human weakness and sinfulness, Christ has sent out certain people to speak his Word and we have to listen to God's Word through those who bring it to us.

I bring up this topic especially because I recently read in the Catholic Telegraph some statistics about the priesthood. I've been quite aware that the Church is losing priests, but the item I am referring to tended to shock me because it was so clear and succinct. Right now there are 180 active priests and 85 retired priests in our archdiocese. In the next five years, 85 priests will become eligible for retirement. If we add in a few that will be ordained and a few who will continue working past retirement, that means that in five years we might have 40 or 50 fewer priests than the 180 we have now. Already many priests are running two parishes. This year we have three being ordained next Saturday. I am simply asking for your continued prayers. Thank you for joining together at the end of Mass each week to pray for vocations to the priesthood and religious life. Please also keep in your prayers those being ordained as well as those older ones like me that we keep our health and energy. I can say that being a priest is not always easy but it is greatly rewarding. Amen.

Fifth Sunday of Easter
May 22, 2011

INTRODUCTION – (Acts 6:1-7; 1 Peter 2:4-9; John 14:1-12) Three weeks ago we heard St. Luke tell us in the Acts of the Apostles how the first Christians got along so harmoniously. Luke tells us they devoted themselves to prayer and instruction from the Apostles and generously shared their material possessions so that no one was in need among them. As the community grew, so did the problems. The very first believers were probably Jews from around Jerusalem who spoke Hebrew or Aramaic. They were culturally and traditionally different from converted Jews who lived in other parts of the Roman Empire and who came to Jerusalem for special occasions. They spoke the common language of the Empire – Greek. They are referred to in today's first reading as the Hellenists. Besides this cultural difference, there were economic issues. Widows in those days were entirely dependent on the community for their basic needs. The Hellenists, those who spoke Greek, complained that their widows were being overlooked when food was being distributed at Christian gatherings. The Apostles felt their role was not to distribute food but to stay focused on prayer and preaching. They solved the problem by creating a new office in the Church, the diaconate.

HOMILY – An elderly couple, admitted by St. Peter through the Pearly Gates, found conditions there just heavenly. The man said to his wife, "I could have been here two years ago if you hadn't fed me all that health food." (*Reader's Digest: Laughter, the Best Medicine*, pg 309)

A priest was going to preach a retreat in a city in Florida. He decided to send a postcard to his mother back home. Walking out of his hotel, he saw a young boy on a bike and asked where the post office was. The boy gave him directions. The priest thanked him and then invited the boy to church that evening. He told him "If you come to church this evening, I'll tell you the way to get to heaven." "I don't think I'll be there," the boy answered. "You don't even know your way to the post office." (Ibidem, pg 312)

The way to heaven is not a street we can walk or drive down. Rand McNally or Google cannot print us a map that will tell us how to get there. The way to heaven is a person; it is Jesus himself – the way, the truth and the life. Through and in Jesus, one comes to eternal glory.

Jesus told his apostles in today's gospel, "If I go and prepare a place for you, I will come back again and take you to myself, so that where I am you also may be." Harold Camping, an 89 year-old evangelist has been telling the world that the Lord would come back again to take his faithful to himself and that the world would end on May 21. Well, here we are. And, well, he is wrong again, just as he has been wrong in his previous predictions. He proclaims himself a prophet, but a real prophet told us: "About that day or hour no one knows, neither the angels in heaven, nor the Son, but only the Father. Beware, keep alert; for you do not know when the time will come." (Mk. 13:32-33) Practically from day one, people have been waiting for our Lord to return and they've been predicting the time and the place, and so far, they've all been wrong. We just have to do what our Lord tells us, "keep alert."

Throughout life we have all learned to deal with the ups and downs of life by keeping before our imagination the big picture. By "big picture" I would like to give three examples of what I mean. Whether a child is practicing the piano or practicing hitting a baseball, they picture themselves performing well someday (keeping in mind the big picture). Whether a parent is going to work every day or trying to teach their child or children the difference between right and wrong, they picture the day when their child or children will be grown, successfully earning a living, perhaps married and raising a family of their own. When I was in the seminary studying hard, trying to survive on seminary cooking, getting up at 6:30 every morning and trying to pray while I was half asleep, I constantly reminded myself my calling in life was not to be a seminarian all my life. I knew someday all my effort would pay off and I would be able to serve God helping people. The big picture. It motivates us, it helps keep us balanced in good times and bad.

Today Jesus is giving us the big, big picture. He begins and ends this short teaching at the Last Supper with the need to have faith. He knew how devastating it would be for his disciples, who had placed so much faith and hope in him, to see him condemned, tortured and crucified. Yet he tells them not to let their hearts be troubled. They must have faith – in God and in him. He tells them he's just going away for a little while and then he's going to come back and take them to be with himself. All the ups and downs we face each day have a purpose, but this is our ultimate purpose, our everlasting goal, enjoying eternal life with our Lord and God. This passage is very comforting to people when they lose someone they love and I have read it and preached on it hundreds of times. It's the really big picture. It's the purpose for which we were created. It's the reason Jesus died on the cross. It's the hope we celebrate now as we come together in prayer, trusting in God's love and uniting ourselves with Jesus in his sacrifice of love for us. Amen.

Sixth Sunday of Easter
May 29, 2011

INTRODUCTION – (Acts 8:5-8, 14-17; 1 Peter 3:15-18; John 14:15-21) St. Luke's Acts of the Apostles tells us how the message of Christ spread throughout the Mediterranean world, starting at Jerusalem. The power behind this growth was the Holy Spirit and the risen (yet invisible) presence of our Lord. As the ministry grew, the Apostolic leaders needed more helpers and so last week they chose seven other men who were ordained to serve, men we now call deacons. Initially they helped with the daily distribution of food to the poor and widows, but it wasn't long before they were preaching the gospel of Christ. The first martyr was one of these seven, St. Steven, who spoke with such power that the enemies of Christ could not contradict him but could only destroy him. Another one of the deacons, Philip, was the first to announce the good news of the resurrection of Jesus in Samaria. The Samaritans were hostile to the Jews and vice versa, but the gospel was well received. The Apostles 'confirm' the ministry of Philip with an even greater outpouring of the gifts of the Holy Spirit.

HOMILY – Some of you may have heard this funny story: it's a letter an old lady wrote to her friend. She said she found a bumper sticker that said: "Honk if you love Jesus." Being very religious she put it on her car. On the way home she stopped at a red light and was lost in thought of how good God is. She didn't know the light had changed, but she was grateful the person behind her loved Jesus, because if he hadn't honked, she wouldn't have noticed the light changed. As a matter of fact, she discovered a lot of people loved Jesus. Her spirits soared being surrounded by such loving people and so she leaned out the window and waved and smiled at all of them. She even honked her horn to be able to share in all that love. She saw a man waving back with only one finger stuck up in the air. She asked her teen-aged grandson in the back seat of the car what that meant. He said it was a Hawaiian good luck sign. Well she just gave him a good luck sign back. She saw her grandson was laughing so hard, and she knew he must have just been filled with the joy of the Spirit. A couple of people got out of their cars and were walking toward her. They probably wanted to pray with her, but just at that moment she noticed the light had turned green so she waved to all of them and drove on. She was the only car to get through the intersection, because the light turned red again and she was sad to have to leave all those loving people – but she gave them one last wave with the Hawaiian good luck sign and drove on.

Jesus tells us today, "If you love me you will keep my commandments." He says it again at the end of this short passage "Whoever has my commandments and observes them is the one who loves me." Anyone can put a bumper sticker on their car. Keeping the commandments is far more challenging. Why is this so important to Jesus? It's because when we don't keep his commandments, we negate his work, we make his life and death meaningless. For that was his work, the meaning of his whole life, to teach us, to lead us and guide us. If we say his teaching has no impact on me, I make up my own rules, we're saying his life has no impact on me; and if his life has no impact on me how can we say we love him. It is a contradiction.

The reward for following his commandments, the reward to letting him be truly Lord in our lives is that he will come into us. He will not leave us orphans, he will come to us, he will live in us. It's wonderful how this works, the more we obey him the more we come to love him. The more we love him, the more we desire to do what he wants of us. Love is not measured by what we feel (although it is nice to experience the joy of being near the one we love – and that's what heaven will be forever) but in this world feelings come and go. Love is measured by what we do. It's all so simple.

It's so important too. Jesus spent the last evening with his Apostles at the Last Supper and he poured out his heart to them, trying to remind them of the most important things he tried to teach them before he would be physically gone from them. Even then, he would be with them in spirit, and through his Holy Spirit, would continue leading them to himself and to the Father. The world, the flesh and the devil do their best to lure us further from God, so it's good to have the extra help of the Spirit to lead us rightly. We feel good when we follow his way and we will rejoice forever for having done so. Amen

Seventh Sunday of Easter
May 16, 1999

HOMILY – (Acts 1:12-14, 1 Pet 4:13-16, John 17:1-11a) Jesus was asked one time what is the most important commandment in the law. We know how he answered. He not only gave us the most important commandment but the second most important commandment as well, two commands that perfectly compliment each other: to love God with our whole heart and soul and mind and strength and to love our neighbor as ourselves. Jesus gave us the answer not only by his words but also by the way he lived.

I would like to reflect today on how Jesus showed love for his Father. His perfect obedience was one way he showed his love. Another way he showed it was by spending time with his Father in prayer. That is what I especially want to focus on today. The topic of prayer was inspired by today's gospel which is part of Jesus prayer at the Last Supper. We have little or no information about what his life was like before he began his public ministry. The little information we do have shows us that Joseph and Mary were faithful in their Jewish observances. Thus Jesus would have been brought up in that tradition, going to synagogue on the Sabbath and going to the Temple in Jerusalem annually for Passover. St. Luke tells us that when Jesus was beginning his ministry he went to Nazareth and went to the synagogue on the Sabbath "according to his custom." Synagogue services would have been very similar to the first part of our Mass. There would be common prayer and readings from the Law and the prophets and with a commentary after each reading. St. Luke points out in his gospel that Jesus was praying as John the Baptist baptized him. Immediately after that, recall how Jesus went into the desert for 40 days to fast and pray. His encounter with the devil there showed he knew the scriptures well and he could quote them easily. Frequently it is mentioned that during his public ministry Jesus was at the Temple participating in liturgical celebrations there. The gospels tell us about Jesus getting up early in the morning to pray or staying up all night in prayer. He would spend time in prayer before important decisions or important events. One time after seeing Jesus praying, the disciples asked him to teach them to pray and of course we are all familiar with the prayer he taught them. In addition to the Our Father, Jesus taught a lot about prayer. For example the parable of a man who had a friend visit him at night and he went to his neighbor to borrow some food, and he kept on knocking until he got what he needed. That's the way Jesus said we should pray. Even when he wasn't teaching about prayer, his teachings reflect the deep relationship Jesus had with his Father. There is no doubt about it, prayer played a major role in Jesus life. The Last Supper of course was more than an ordinary supper. It was the Passover which Jesus was celebrating with his disciples, which was a religious celebration.

His prayer (in the 17th chapter of John) is divided into three parts. First Jesus prays for himself, then for his apostles, then for all who would come to believe in him. Notice how many times the word "glory" is used in today's gospel. Jesus saw his death and resurrection as a moment of glory, a moment when God's saving love would be revealed to the world. He prays that the Father might be glorified in all that was to take place and that in the fulfillment of his mission, he might be a source of life for all who would believe in him. It is comforting to know he prayed for all of us at the Last Supper. He continues to intercede for us each time we celebrate the Lord's Supper.

There is not the time to analyze this prayer thoroughly. My main point today was simply to point out the prayerfulness of Jesus. We see in the first reading how Jesus followers imitated his example as they gathered together in prayer in the upper room after the Ascension, waiting for the coming of the Holy Spirit.

Louis Evely in his book, *Teach us to Pray*, wrote: "Too many Christians regard God as pilots regard their parachute, namely, good if needed, but better if they can get along without it." We might wonder why would Jesus need to pray? He was already as close to the Father as he possibly could be. I am sure there are many reasons why Jesus prayed, but this question might best be answered with another question: "why do we need to spend time with those who are important to us, with those whom we love?"

A true disciple of our Lord will make prayer a priority in their lives, and by "prayer" I mean more than just a rapidly recited Our Father or Hail Mary. Prayer is spending time with our God. Do we feel like we're too busy? I will never forget what our spiritual director in the seminary told us. The busier we are the more we need to pray.

Today we come together for the greatest prayer there is. As we gather in prayer today, we are not alone and I don't mean simply that there are others here in church with us. Christ is with us and it is in union with his perfect sacrifice of love and obedience on the cross that we offer our prayers and praise to God our Father.

Feast of the Ascension
June 5, 2011

HOMILY – (Acts 1:1-11; Ephesians 1:17-23; Matthew 28:16-20) During June a lot of people get married. So I have three stories about marriage:

1) A little boy asked his father "Daddy, how much does it cost to get married? Dad replied, "I don't know, son. I'm still paying."

2) A lady put an ad in the newspaper that read, "Husband wanted." The next day she got 200 answers to her ad. They all said the same thing, "You can have mine."

3) A husband read an article to his wife about how many words women use a day as opposed to how many words men say; – 30,000 to a man's 15,000. The wife replied, "The reason has to be because we have to repeat everything to men." The husband turned to his wife and said: "What?"

Besides being the feast of the Ascension, today is also the feast of St. Boniface. St. Boniface does not quite generate the kind of celebration that is usually associated with St. Patrick (whether that's good or bad, I cannot say). However, Boniface is as important to Germany as Patrick was to Ireland. When Boniface was sent to Germany, it was mostly pagan. Even the Christianity that was there was mixed with paganism. For 35 years he worked tirelessly trying to reform the Church in Germany, to educate the clergy, and to bring the people back to fidelity to the Holy Father. It was not as glorious a task as bringing people to Christ who had never heard of him (which is what Patrick did), but Boniface had the hard work of correcting and rejuvenating the faith of those who already thought they had the faith and who thought they didn't need renewal. Learning something for the first time is easier than having to unlearn what is erroneous and then learning what is correct. Often I am asked about the stained glass window we have of Boniface cutting down the tree. That tree was considered sacred to the pagan gods and everyone thought he would be struck dead if he cut it down. Those who were nearby were pagan priests apparently waiting for lightening to strike – but Boniface cut it down without anything happening. It split into four parts when it fell and he was able to use the wood to build a chapel. He not only worked in Germany but in France and in the Netherlands too. After 35 years of service to God, Boniface, along with 53 companions, were attacked and massacred by pagans on their way to the Netherlands for a Confirmation. Thus he is a martyr, his red garb symbolizes that, and we would normally wear red on his feast, but the feast of the Ascension is what we are celebrating today.

The Ascension celebrates Jesus' glorification far above every being that could be named in this age and in the one to come (as Paul says in today's second reading). As we profess each week, Jesus ascended into heaven and is seated at the right hand of the Father. It is not the end of his work. He tells his disciples in today's gospel, "I will be with you always, until the end of time." He showed he was with them by how the Church grew through the teaching of the apostles, through the miracles they worked and through the courage he gave them – even giving them courage to face martyrdom for their faith.

His ascension to glory is something beyond our human abilities to understand. That is what is symbolized by the cloud that took him from their sight. yet, when Jesus' risen body entered into the world of the divine he gave us hope, for he promised us, "I am going to get a place ready for you and I will come back and take you with me, that where I am, you also may be." (John 14:3)

If we try to pinpoint the exact day for the Ascension we are unable to do so. Mark, Luke and John give us the impression in their gospels that Jesus ascended to the Father on Easter Sunday night. Luke, who also wrote the Acts of the Apostles, tells us the ascension took place 40 days after Easter. Forty is a round number that is used frequently in the Bible to give us a rough idea of how much time had passed by. Scholars tell us the ascension seems to have taken place in two stages (*The New Jerome Biblical Commentary*, 43:198) This might be a little heavy, so please bear with me. The first stage, which according to the gospels took place on Easter Sunday night, is called the "doxological" account. The Greek word doxa means splendor, glory, honor thus according to the doxological account of the ascension, the disciples encountered Jesus a number of times, they were instructed by him, and worshipped him. Luke describes this phase of the ascension at the end of his gospel by telling us after Jesus blessed the disciples and was parted from them and was taken up to heaven, "they did him homage and then returned to Jerusalem with great joy, and they were continually in the temple praising God." The second stage of the ascension can be called the "ecclesiastical" account. Ecclesia means church thus according to this account the church must move beyond this period of joyful worship and frequent appearances of Jesus and begin to travel the highways of the world with the good news. That is the message of today's gospel from Matthew. Notice in today's gospel, Matthew doesn't even mention the ascension. He wants us not so much to focus on where Jesus went but to focus on what Jesus wants us to do now. St. Luke gives us the same message when the angel asks the disciples, "Why are you standing there looking at the sky?" In other words it's time to get to work boys and girls.

Matthew tells us the apostles would go forth with the Authority of Jesus; they were to go to all the nations; their ministry would be sacramental (they would baptize) and it would be a ministry of teaching people to observe all that I have commanded you. Notice the use of the word "all." "All authority," "all nations," "all that I command," "all days." The mission of the Church (which is our mission today) has no limit. Our patron St. Boniface lived that. May each of us, in our own way, do the same.

Pentecost
June 12, 2011

HOMILY – One Saturday night a minister was busy writing his sermon for Sunday. His little daughter saw him working busily and asked him what he was doing. He said he was writing his sermon. She asked, "Daddy, how do you know what to write?" He answered, "God tells me what to write." Then she asked, "Why do you keep erasing."

Sometimes it's very clear and sometimes it's challenging to know what God is saying to us. I felt pretty much like that minister when I was trying to figure out just what I should say about the coming of the Holy Spirit on Pentecost. So much could be said (I have four or five entire books on the Holy Spirit) and yet, when we finish saying everything that could be said, we will still be dealing with the great mystery of who is the Holy Spirit and the Spirit's mysterious workings in us and in the Church. It's a great mystery because God is too awesome and too great for us to understand.

The theologian, Fr. Yves Congar , has written: "The Spirit is without a face and almost without a name. [The Spirit] is the wind who is not seen, but who makes things move. [The Spirit] is known by [the Spirit's] effects. [The Spirit] is the one who is given in order to produce everything that can be summarized as the community of the sons [and daughters] of God." Simply put: "The Spirit is the agent of the fulfillment of God's plan and work." (*Congar, I Believe in the Spirit*, Vol. 3 pg 144)

As this feast, this gift of the Spirit encompasses so much, I can only mention a few disconnected ideas that I feel deserve some special mention. With the coming of the Spirit the liturgy brings the Easter season to a close.

Although there are two special Sundays after today, the feast of the Holy Trinity and the feast of the Body and Blood of Christ, the liturgical season of Ordinary Time begins Monday.

When God's Spirit came upon the Apostles and disciples, then the Church was born. God's Spirit got things moving like a strong wind, or a fire that could not be stopped, and the Apostles began to preach, starting at Jerusalem and carrying the message of Jesus to the ends of the earth. This last statement, the growth of the Church under the direction of the Spirit, describes the basic theme of the Acts of the Apostles.

The Spirit continues to try to keep the Church united and faithful to its mission. This is one of the things Jesus especially prayed for at the Last Supper – that we all will be one. It's a point St. Paul made in his letter to the Corinthians ("in one Spirit we were all baptized into one body ...") Yet we are divided into so many different versions of Christianity.

Paul has spoken at great length about the activity of the Spirit. He has told us how the Spirit calls individuals to different forms of service or ministry. We had an example of that this week when Joe Binzer was ordained to be bishop in our Archdiocese. He will be helping Archbishop Schnurr. I am very excited about the choice of Bishop Binzer. Before coming to the seminary he was a CPA. His first assignment was in a parish, but in the past eight years he has been Chancellor for the Archdiocese. I've had many contacts with him as Chancellor and he has always been a great help. He has come here many times to help with confessions or to do a wedding. I am sure he will be a great blessing for our Archdiocese. It is not just as a bishop or priest that the Spirit calls people to ministry, and I'm afraid I would bore everyone if I tried to mention all the ways the Spirit inspires people to serve God and the community, either paid or as volunteers. If I did try to name all the different ways people serve, I know I would forget to name some of those ways and then someone would feel unappreciated. You know who you are and can pat yourself on the back.

Actually, I am convinced that everyone here at Mass today is here because they have been moved by the Holy Spirit to be here. Paul said, "no one can say 'Jesus is Lord', except by the Holy Spirit." (1 Cor. 12:3) The Holy Spirit helps us to believe.

Two closing thoughts: Often I have asked people if they belong to any faith, whether they have any religion. They often answer, "We don't believe in organized religion, but we are spiritual people." I never push it but I often wonder what "spiritual" means to them. Anyone who believes in God is spiritual in some sense, whether they are pagans, Hindus or Buddhists or Moslems. Even radical Moslems who go around beheading people in the name of Allah consider themselves spiritual people. Even demons are spiritual because that's what they are made of, spirit. Being spiritual says nothing special about us. What matters is whether we let God's Holy Spirit lead us, God's Holy Spirit who connects us with the Father and with Jesus and who connects us with the community of believers in Christ.

My last comment: When I speak to parents of children who are preparing for the sacrament of Confirmation, I remind them of the fruits of the Holy Spirit as identified by St. Paul. His list begins with love (not just any kind of love, but a generous, giving kind of love). He goes on to mention joy, peace, patience, kindness, generosity, faithfulness, gentleness and self-control. I encourage them to help prepare their children for this sacrament so their children will be abundantly blessed with these qualities. I ask them if they would like to see more of these virtues in their children. I wish to conclude by asking you, wouldn't you like to have more of these virtues in yourself. Let us pray today for greater openness to the Spirit for Jesus tells us: "If you then, who are evil, know how to give good gifts to your children, how much more will the heavenly Father give the Holy Spirit to those who ask him!" (Lk. 11:13).

Feast of the Holy Trinity
June 19, 2011

INTRODUCTION – (Exodus 34:4b-6, 8-9; 2 Corinthians 13:11-13; John 3:16-18) Tertullian first used the word "Trinity" to describe God about the year 200 AD. The council of Nicaea adopted the term 125 years later in formulating the Creed we proclaim each week at Sunday Mass. It took a very long time for the Church Fathers and theologians to clarify this doctrine of the Trinity. There were many reasons that it took such a long time. Among the primary reasons would be 1) that belief in one God was so deeply embedded in the Jewish faith, the faith that gave birth to Christianity and 2) because three persons in one God was such an entirely new and difficult concept.

Today in our first reading we hear about Moses who lived 1300 years before Christ. At that time and for hundreds of years thereafter, all the nations that were part of the Middle East believed in many gods. The Hebrews were different. They believed there is only one God. It was part of their covenant that they worship none of the other gods of their neighbors: I am the Lord thy God, thou shalt not have strange gods before me. In our reading today, we hear God revealing his sacred name to Moses. By giving his name, God is entering into relationship with the Hebrews and making himself accessible to them. In the Hebrew bible, that name is spelled YHWH, but it was never pronounced. That is because the Jews were afraid of even the slightest risk of using God's sacred name in vain (which the second commandment forbad). So whenever YHWH came up in the text, they always substituted the title "Lord" as we hear in today's first reading. God's self-revelation to Moses in today's reading is that God is merciful and gracious, slow to anger and rich in kindness and fidelity; characteristics of God that appear also in today's gospel. It is interesting that those who espouse inclusive language in today's politically correct society like to call God "he/she" yet they have no difficulty referring to the devil as "he."

HOMILY – Three boys were bragging about their fathers. The first boasted that his dad owned a farm. The second said his dad owned a factory. The third boy, a pastor's son, replied: "That's nothin'. My dad owns hell." "No way!" one of the boys said. "Nobody can own hell." The preacher's son said, "Well, my dad does. I heard mom tell grandma that the church council gave it to him last night." (*Joyful Noiseletter*, June-July, 1994, pg 2)

A small boy who had been a Dennis the Menace all day was saying bedtime prayers with his dad. After a short prayer, the little boy asked his dad to leave him alone so he could talk to God by himself. Dad asked, "What have you done that you don't want me to know about." "If I tell you," the boy said, "you'll get angry and shout and yell, but God will listen, forgive me and forget about it." (Ibidem, pg 2) The parable of the Prodigal Son (also sometimes called the parable of the Prodigal Father) somewhat resembles that story. Happy Fathers' Day to all our fathers – whether actual fathers or those who play the role of father in someone's life.

Today we reflect on one of the basic mysteries of our faith, the Holy Trinity. One of the most important things about a mystery is that we can know some things about it but we cannot understand it fully. That is the way the Trinity has always been and always will be as long as we live in this world. God is too great for our minds to understand. It should not be a mystery to us that God is too great for us to fully understand for we could only fully understand God if we were on the same level as God is, and we're not. In God's kingdom we will see God as God is and then we will not need to understand for we will be captivated by all that God is and we will be filled with enough awe and love to last us forever.

I could talk for a long time or for a short time, but I could never explain this mystery. We have to take it on faith, a faith which has Jesus Christ for its foundation. It is from Jesus we have learned of the Father and the Spirit and it is from him that we have learned that he and the Father are one (John 10:30). It is from him we have learned that "he who sees me sees also the Father." (John 14:9) It is by his command that we have been baptized "in the name of the Father and of the Son and of the Holy Spirit." He taught us to call God our Father. Of course, we can pray to any one of the three persons, or we can pray to all three persons at once as we do at Mass. At Mass we direct our prayers to the Father through our Lord, Jesus Christ, who lives and reigns with the Father and the Holy Spirit, one God, forever and ever.

As I'm sure most of you know, there are going to be some changes in the words of the prayers we say at Mass. These changes attempt to improve and refine the translation of the Mass that was made after Vatican II. Our creed will be changed from "we believe" to "I believe." It is still the faith of the entire Church, but it stresses our own personal profession of that faith. It also is similar to the "I believe" which begins the Apostles Creed, an expression of our faith that goes back almost to the time of the Apostles. Now we say we believe that Jesus is "one in being with the Father." A more precise theological term will be introduced here: Jesus is "consubstantial with the Father." This means he is of the same substance or the same essence as the Father. It stresses more clearly Jesus' divinity. Another more precise theological term we will soon use is to say that Jesus was "incarnate of the Virgin Mary" rather than saying Jesus was "born of the Virgin Mary". This is saying that the Son of God, who was divine from all eternity, took on our human flesh at the moment of his conception when the angel appeared to Mary and said she would conceive by the power of the Holy Spirit. This just gives you a tiny view of what is ahead, but don't get nervous, there are not a lot of big words that will be unfamiliar to us. I wanted to mention this because I was talking about the creed. The Trinity is a mystery for us now, but rest assured, the time will come when it will all make sense and the joy it will bring us will be fantastic. Amen.

The Body and Blood of Christ
June 26, 2011

INTRODUCTION – (Deuteronomy 8:2-3, 14b-16a; 1 Corinthians 10:16-17; John 6:51-58) The setting for our first reading is on the east side of the Jordan River across from the Promised Land. Moses' job of leading the people of God is just about finished. He is giving them some last minute instructions before they cross the Jordan and enter the Land and he goes off to his eternal reward. His fear is that the people, once they get comfortable in this new land, will become complacent and forget the God on whom they depend. So he tells them to remember – remember the journey from Egypt, remember the long time they spent in the desert and especially remember the food with which God fed them – the manna. This reading (especially the mention of manna) is meant to introduce us to the main focus of today's feast – how God sustains us with the flesh and blood of his Son, Jesus, the bread of life.

HOMILY – A tough old cowboy told his grandson that the secret to long life was sprinkling a little gunpowder on his oatmeal every morning. The grandson did this religiously and, sure enough, lived to the ripe old age of 93. When he died, he left behind 10 children, 28 grandchildren, 35 great grandchildren and a 15-foot hole in the wall of the crematorium. (from *Reader's Digest, Laughter, the Best Medicine*, pg. 199)

There's even a better secret to a long life than putting gunpowder on your breakfast cereal: it is Jesus' teaching about eternal life in today's gospel.

Imagine that you went to your doctor for a routine physical. The doctor saw some things she was concerned about and sent you to get some tests. The tests came back with very bad news. The doctor told you that the tests showed you would have only about six months to live and the tests were highly reliable and accurate. But the doctor said she has discovered a special medicine that would cure the problem. She promised you if you took this medicine, a medicine with no troubling side effects, you would in all likelihood enjoy good health for another 20 or 30 years. You've known your doctor for years, you know she is very knowledgeable and you've always trusted her. How much time would you spend dealing with all the doubts that flood your mind? Would you be foolish to trust or foolish not to trust? What you decide to do may all come down to that: trust.

Jesus tells us in today's gospel, if we want to live forever, we must eat his body and drink his blood. Would we be foolish to trust what he tells us or foolish not to trust it. The Jews who first heard him asked: "How can that be?" A reasonable question! We still ask it. But the answer is beyond reason, it is answered only by faith. Jesus said it and he said it in the clearest possible terms. When his hearers questioned him, he repeated what he had said and said it more emphatically: "Amen, amen, I say to you (whenever he prefixes a statement with 'Amen, amen' he's saying this is really serious). Then he said "unless you eat the flesh of the Son of Man and drink his blood, you do not have life within you."

If you look up today's gospel passage in your Bibles, you will see that after Jesus insisted we must eat his body and drink his blood in order to have eternal life, many of his followers started walking away, saying to themselves that he was out of his mind. What is important here is what Jesus didn't do. The gospel tells us he didn't call them back. He didn't say, "wait, don't take me literally." He didn't say, "you misunderstand me – I don't mean you really have to eat my body and drink my blood." Jesus just let them go; he knew they understood him perfectly.

The apostles, however, stayed with him even though they didn't understand what he was saying any more than anyone else. When Jesus asked them, "Do you also want to leave?" Peter answered: "Lord, to whom shall we go? You have the words of eternal life."

It is quite marvelous how Jesus devised a way to feed us with his own flesh and blood. He has given us the Eucharist, which is his real presence. The Eucharist is truly his body and blood. Yet it remains a mystery for us and we are still asking, "How can this be?" It all comes down to faith, faith in the one who tells us, "This is my body. This is my blood."

I think this is the biggest challenge to our faith in the Church today. It is also the biggest comfort to those who believe. Once we are truly convinced that the Eucharist is Jesus' body and blood, then it is much easier for us to see how it is the source of eternal life for us. Jesus gave us a simple image to help us see how, through the Eucharist, he brings us eternal life. He told us, "I am the vine, you are the branches." By our union with him which endures and is nourished through the Eucharist, his divine life flows into us.

Moses told God's people not to forget what God had done for them. Today's feast inspires us not to forget what Jesus does and continues to do for us through the Eucharist. Amen.

Feast of St. Peter & St. Paul
June 29, 2008

INTRODUCTION – (Acts 12: 1-11, 2 Timothy 4: 6-8, 17-18, Matthew 16:13-19) **At 4:00 Mass:** Christ continues to feed and guide his people through the apostles. We see today how he does this through two of them, Peter and Paul. Peter, in today's first reading, shows us Jesus at work through him and John in healing a person crippled from birth. Peter's position as leader and chief shepherd of God's people is recognized in today's gospel. This was written long after Peter had been put to death, so it is not just Peter who is appointed chief shepherd, but those who would succeed him. We hear from St. Paul in the second reading. Paul was a powerful teacher and his mission was, to a large part, to the Gentiles. He recognized that fidelity to Christ did not require Gentiles to observe all of Jewish law with its feasts and rituals and sacrifices and dietary requirements. In today's second reading he is assuring his readers that he teaches with divine authority and has received backing from Peter (Cephas) and the other leaders of the early Church.

At Sunday Masses:

A society cannot survive without structure, organization and authority. Today's feast of the apostles, Peter and Paul, especially today's gospel, reminds us of the way Christ structured his Church with Peter as the head. When we hear this gospel, it might be worth knowing that it was written after Peter had already been put to death. St. Matthew wants us to know that it was a leadership position Jesus was creating when he made Peter the rock and gave him the keys of the kingdom. It was not just a personal prerogative of Peter's. If it were personal only to Peter, who was dead by the time Matthew was writing, why would St. Matthew have made so much of it in his gospel?

I would like you to notice also in today's readings the theme of God helping those who put their trust in him. The first reading tells us how God rescued Peter from prison. The psalm that follows is the prayer of a person praising God for rescuing them from fear and danger. We could easily imagine Peter praying this psalm as he left prison. In the second reading Paul realizes he is approaching the end of his life and he praises God for all the ways he has been protected during his ministry.

HOMILY – Today we celebrate the feast of Saints Peter and Paul. It is a very ancient feast going back to around the year 250 A.D. The two are honored because they are the two apostles about whom we know the most. They were the greatest influence on the Church at its beginning. Tradition has it they died together in Rome during the persecution of the Emperor Nero. Most historians suspect that Nero himself started the fire that burned most of Rome in order to clear out old houses and buildings to make room for his own ambitious building projects. Then he blamed the fire on the Christians in order to take suspicion off himself.

Peter was crucified upside down, again tradition has it that he did not consider himself worthy of dying in the same way his Master had died. Paul was beheaded. Although he was a Jew, he also was legally, by birth, a Roman citizen. Roman law decreed that Roman citizens could not be crucified because it was such a horrific way to die and being exempt from crucifixion was one of the perks of being a Roman citizen.

This year the spotlight is on St. Paul because the Holy Father proclaimed that the rest of this year and the first six months of next year be a year in honor of St. Paul. No one knows when he was born exactly, but scholars figure it was roughly 2000 years ago (give or take three or four years). So we are celebrating his 2000th birthday as closely as we can figure it.

We don't know if Paul ever saw Jesus in the flesh. Paul was born in Tarsus, a city in Asia Minor, which is now modern day Turkey. He spoke Greek and Aramaic and wrote all of his letters in Greek. He was a Pharisee and 1000% dedicated to observance of Jewish law and traditions. Sometime after the death and resurrection of Jesus, he began persecuting the early followers of Christ. He was present at the martyrdom of St. Steven, the first martyr. He viewed those who believed in Jesus as heretics. He was such a zealous devotee to the Jewish Law that he would go looking for believers in Jesus to arrest them and prosecute them. It was on such a journey to Damascus that the Risen Christ spoke to Paul. Paul was enveloped in a bright light and fell to the ground. There is no mention of a horse, although people are used to saying he was thrown off his horse. This idea came from a painting of the event. I rather believe Paul was walking or riding a donkey, which was the usual means of transportation. He heard someone call him, and when he asked who was calling him, Jesus answered: "I am Jesus whom you are persecuting." Then Jesus said: "Now get up and go into the city and you will be told what you must do." Paul got up but he was a new man. He was ill and blind for a few days until he was healed by one of Jesus' followers and was baptized. In his encounter with Jesus, he discovered Jesus was not a heretic and condemned criminal, but the glorified Lord who has risen from the dead and lives in his Church. He would learn that his mission would be to the Gentiles and that the good news Jesus proclaimed was to be preached to all people. This is when Paul became an Apostle for the word Apostle means one who has been sent. He would come to understand how we are saved by Jesus' death and resurrection and by our incorporation into this saving event through three things: 1) faith, 2) the sacraments, especially baptism and the Eucharist and 3) our love for one another.

Paul wrote more than any other New Testament author. One could keep on talking about him because he wrote so much. There is an insert in today's bulletin that says more about Paul. But to put everything succinctly, Paul's life and mission can be summed up in the one sentence Jesus spoke to him on the way to Damascus: "I am Jesus whom you are persecuting."

As I conclude, we might recall the most famous lines Paul wrote: "love is kind, love is patient, love is not jealous, it is not pompous, etc." ending with the sentence: "love never fails." The kind of love Paul talks about is a love that is rooted in Christ. We express that love as we gather here in faith today, giving God our time and worship and praying for one another. May we continue to express that same love for one another throughout the coming week.

Fourteenth Sunday in Ordinary Time
July 3, 2011

INTRODUCTION – (Zechariah 9:9-10; Romans 8:9, 11-13; Matthew 11:25-30) Two hundred thirty-five years ago, we declared our independence from the English. This was a courageous step on the part of our ancestors and it has been challenged in many ways through these years. Somehow we have managed to keep going, and with God's blessings, we will continue on. May we use our freedom with responsibility and may God bless our land.

Two hundred thirty-five years is a long time. When we hear from Zechariah in today's first reading, it had been three hundred years since the Jews had enjoyed freedom. First they were under the brutal exile of the Babylonians for 50 years until the Persians destroyed the Babylonian empire and allowed the Jews to return to their homes. Alexander the Great conquered the Persians and eventually, during this Hellenistic period, the Jews were bitterly persecuted. Scholars believe that it was during this period of Greek rule that Zechariah, as God's prophet, promises better days. He tells Jerusalem to rejoice for their king would come to bring them freedom and peace. Since kings were anointed, they were called in Hebrew "Messiah" and in Greek "Christos" which means "the anointed one." Horses, chariots, warriors' bows and other instruments of war would be outlawed in his kingdom. The people of Jerusalem remembered this prophecy when Jesus came riding into Jerusalem on a donkey on Palm Sunday. We hear, in today's gospel, Jesus reveals himself as a man of peace who is meek and humble of heart. That's why the passage from Zechariah was chosen for our first reading. Someday, after we learn to better follow Jesus, the man of peace, maybe we will then see Zechariah's prophecy of peace fulfilled fully.

HOMILY – A man came home from a long day of counting ballots at the Board of Elections in his area. He said to his wife, "We won, dear. I'm now a state representative." Not sure she heard correctly, she said "Honestly!" He said in reply, "now don't bring anything up about honesty!"

Some of you may have heard this true story. It was at a graduation ceremony at the University of Maryland a few years ago. The graduates marched in with great solemnity. Parents were smiling and brushing away tears at the same time. The speakers appropriately stayed within the guidelines of political correctness and no one dared ask for divine blessings on the graduates or their families. The final speaker, one of the students, went to the podium, he stood there silently for a few moments then, without a cue, every one of the graduates sneezed. The student at the podium looked at the audience and said, "God bless you, each and every one of you." And he walked off the stage. The audience exploded into applause.

So, on this holiday weekend, I say God bless each and every one of you. We know our country is not perfect, nor are all its politicians, but it's the best country on the face of the earth. Just the fact that we are here today is one indication of that. In some countries our lives would be threatened or we would be put in jail just for doing what we're doing. Let us continue to work and pray that we might remain strong, able to stand on our own, and remain free – not to do just anything we feel like, but free to serve God and to serve each other in love.

Friday was the feast of the Sacred Heart of Jesus. I mention that because the gospel for that feast is the same gospel we just heard today. "Come to me," Jesus said, "and I will give you rest. Take my yoke upon you and learn from me for I am meek and humble of heart. ..."

The Sacred Heart is a special symbol of Jesus' love for us. We must not forget Jesus had (and has) a human heart just as we do. St. Paul said he became like us in all things except sin. He feels emotions of love, compassion and tenderness. Because when we love someone, we want to be loved back, he also feels it when we forget him, betray him, do what displeases him. Joined to that human heart is the infinite love of God. Thus when we see a statue or picture of the Sacred Heart, there are usually flames of fire coming from it representing the immense love of God. Because God is love, as St. John tells us, Jesus cannot not love, even when we refuse him our love. So he asks special people to offer him greater love to make up for the pain of what he suffered for us, the pain of rejected love. That is the meaning of the crown of thorns we see surrounding Jesus' heart. This is, in essence, the theme of devotion to the Sacred Heart: 1) recognizing Jesus love and 2) offering repentance for the love that we and others have failed to give him. This is the reason we have First Friday Mass and why we have holy hours. This is the reason ultimately for the Eucharist itself. There are many blessings Jesus promised to those who honor him as the Sacred Heart.

Jesus said, "come to me." "Come" is the word I want to stress here. He has already come to us, through his birth, his teachings and miracles, his death and resurrection, through grace and the sacraments. He has come as far as possible. Coming to him implies we have to move closer, we have more we have to learn from him. We have to take time to pray, to read the Scriptures, to forgive those who have hurt us, to be kind to others and all the other things we've been taught about living a life of holiness. Don't expect that Jesus is going to make us rich and take all our problems away. He did promise a cross to those who follow him. Life itself, however, has many crosses, whether we follow Jesus or not. It's a lot easier when we have Jesus as part of our everyday lives. "My yoke is easy and my burden light." "Come to me all you who labor and are burdened." Amen.

Fifteenth Sunday in Ordinary Time
July 10, 2011

INTRODUCTION – (Isaiah 55:10-11; Romans 8:18-23; Matthew 13:1-9 or 1-23) In today's first reading, the prophet had as his audience God's captive people in Babylon. God had been telling them, through the prophet, that after 50 years of captivity and slavery to the Babylonians, they would soon be able to return to Israel, to their cities, their homes and their farms. Many doubted this could be true. In today's passage God is assuring them his promise will be fulfilled. God compares his word to the rain and the snow. When God sends moisture to the earth, it does the work of keeping the world green and alive. When God sends out his word, it is not full of empty promises, it is effective and powerful and is able to accomplish what it was sent to do. As we will hear in today's gospel parable, another way of thinking of the power of the word of God is to think of it as a seed.

HOMILY – A newly ordained priest was having a

difficult time getting started preparing his first sermon. He asked his pastor for a suggestion and his pastor told him: "start with something that's certain to grab their attention. For example, you might say: 'some of the best years of my life were spent in the arms of a woman who was someone else's wife." The pastor smiled at the young priest's shocked expression, then added "She was my mother." That Sunday the nervous young priest ascended the pulpit, sweating and shaking. Finally he said "the pastor told me some of the best years of his life were spent in the arms of a woman who was someone else's wife." He was pleased in getting everyone's attention but his nervousness overtook him, his mind went blank and he just blurted out: "For the life of me, I can't remember if he said who she was." (*Reader's Digest, Laughter*, pg 285)

I thought that might be an appropriate start for today's parable about growth. As infants we all spent a lot of time in someone's arms, most probably our parents. But somehow we grew up, started walking, talking, going to school, then eventually driving, working, getting married perhaps and getting older. When we were young, we couldn't grow up fast enough; now time goes by too fast.

Counting this Sunday's parable, we're going to have three weeks of parables about God's kingdom (or as Matthew likes to call it: "the kingdom of heaven"). Actually today's parable is hardly a parable. A parable usually has an unexpected ending. Today's parable is entirely predictable. If we throw seed on the ground, some of it will grow if the climate is agreeable and there is enough sun and moisture. I used the short form of the parable because we've heard it so often and pretty much know how it is interpreted. If we were reading Matthew's gospel from beginning to end, we would see that today's gospel describes the various ways people had been responding to Jesus up to this point in his ministry. He was accused of being possessed, of being a breaker of divine law, and a blasphemer. Some people thought he was a great healer, and having made them well, they went happily on about their business and didn't think any more about him. Some enjoyed his stories and were entertained as long as he was willing to entertain them, but if he asked something difficult of them, they sought other kinds of entertainment. Then there were some who thought he had something worthwhile to say and they continued to listen to him and learn from him. Jesus was like the farmer sowing the seed. Although he didn't touch all hearts, those whose hearts he touched grew and produced good fruit; that is, their lives were virtuous and pleasing to God.

Jesus' message for us in today's parable is to know first of all that the kingdom of heaven is not an entitlement (as a lot of people these days assume it is). Just because the seed of grace has been planted in our hearts, if we do nothing with it, it will die. If it lives in us, it will grow. We know that some of the growth we experience in life, such as growing physically, just happens automatically as we grow older. Other kinds of growth require intentional effort on our part – such as growing in enough knowledge to get a degree or growing in certain skills; i.e., athletic or artistic or knowing how to get along socially with others or managing our finances so we can support ourselves.

Growing in God's grace and holiness is like this second kind of growth. It is intentional on our part. It is not accidental. It involves making a choice that Jesus is more important to us than anything or anyone else. It means choosing to believe that he has come to teach us the way to God and choosing to follow him faithfully. It also involves patience as we wait for the fullness of the kingdom. Just as God has given us the sun and the rain to make the seed grow, so if we put forth the effort spiritually, God will supply the means necessary to produce an extraordinarily abundant harvest in our lives. Investing our lives in him will give us a fantastic return on our investment (30, 60 or 100 fold).

Sixteenth Sunday in Ordinary Time
July 17, 2011

INTRODUCTION – (Wisdom 12:13, 16-19; Romans 8:26-27; Matthew 13:24-43) The first reading today could be difficult to follow. It is from the book of Wisdom, a book of the bible written about 100 years before Christ. At the time, the Jews were being persecuted for their faith. Many Jews were giving up their belief in God and converting to pagan ways. The author of this book is struggling with the question: "why is God allowing this evil to go on?" His conclusion is that God's power is not directed toward destroying evil people, but in showing patience, wanting people to repent and allowing them time to do so. This theme prepares us for the gospel, which also deals with the problem of evil.

HOMILY – A man was suffering from a serious attack of appendicitis. He hated going to the doctor, but his wife would not let him suffer. Finally she got him to a doctor who arranged for an operation. Still in pain and still protesting the idea of an operation, he said to the doctor, "When God gave people an appendix, there must have been a reason for putting it in our bodies." "Oh, there was," said the doctor. "God gave you that appendix so I could put my children through college." (from *Reader's Digest: Laughter, the Best Medicine*, pg 308)

People of faith tend to believe that God has a reason

for everything, even if that reason is not obvious. Sometimes people can't figure out God's plans. They give up trying to understand and decide either God doesn't have any plans or God doesn't have any control or simply they decide there is no God. Most atheists have come to the belief that there is no God because of the problem of evil in the world. Their argument is if there is a good God, then God would not allow all the evil we see. He would stop it, but since there is so much evil, there must not be a good God. Their argument ignores all the good things we see in our world, which far outweigh the evil.

Our first reading from the Book of Wisdom and Jesus' parable of the wheat and the weeds gives us one way to help us understand the problem of evil. It is that God is patient while waiting and urging the evil doers to change their ways. We've all gotten impatient with God at times, thinking God is too patient. In the end, aren't we grateful that God is patient for we're all sinners and we have all failed at times. We all try to be the good element (the wheat) in God's kingdom. Otherwise we wouldn't be here today. In the course of our lives, if we're honest, we know we haven't been perfect all the time. Thankfully, God is patient and God is merciful. God wishes none to perish as he tells us in the parable of the lost sheep. (Mt. 18:14) Today's parable though seems to tell us clearly that some will not be saved.

Jesus' parable last week, the three today, and the three next week are about one of his favorite topics – the kingdom of heaven. The kingdom is the "good news" that Jesus preached. John the Baptist preached about it before him. They both preached that it was near. Yet Jesus also implied it's coming was off in the future (how far off, no one knows) for he taught us to pray for its coming ("thy kingdom come"). Like the seed in the gospel, it has been planted, it has begun, but it has not fully arrived. It comes about slowly, but the harvest will inevitably come. Jesus preached over and over we can choose on which side we will be at the end. If we want to be on his good side, we must live what he has preached. He loves each of us with a love beyond what we can imagine and wants us to share eternal life with him. That's why he came to us, that's why he died for us, that's why he gives himself to us now as we gather in prayer and receive him in the Eucharist.

The end result of Jesus' work will be huge. That's the point of the other two parables, the mustard seed (as small as a fly spec on a piece of paper) or a little yeast kneaded into a big batch of flour. Even though Jesus started his community of believers with a handful of people, today there are over two billion people who identify themselves as Christians. Even though not always recognized, God's kingdom is real. He wants us to be part of it and to share in all its blessings because he loves us. Amen

Seventeenth Sunday in Ordinary Time
July 24, 2011

INTRODUCTION – (1 Kings 3:5, 7-12; Romans 8:28-30; Matthew 13:44-52) When King David died, his son, Solomon, succeeded him as king of Israel. Today's first reading is Solomon's prayer as he begins his reign. He prayed for an understanding heart that he would reign well. Of all the possible gifts he could have asked for, he chose to ask for wisdom. Observance of God's commands will lead us to wisdom, thus in our reflection on our first reading we praise God in the psalm refrain for his commands and for the wisdom they impart to us.

HOMILY – A junior manager, a senior manager, and their boss were in a cab on their way to a lunch meeting. There in the cab they found a lamp and rubbed it. Out came a genie who said, "I'll grant you one wish each." The senior manager spoke up first: "I want to be on a fast boat in the Bahamas with no worries." And poof, he was gone. The junior manager couldn't contain his excitement and shouted, "I want to be in Miami, with beautiful girls, food and cocktails." And poof, he was gone. Finally, it was the boss's turn who stated emphatically: "I want those idiots back in the office after lunch." (from *Reader's Digest: Laughter, the Best Medicine*, pg 345)

When God offered Solomon anything he wanted, he chose wisdom, but he didn't put it to good use. He was involved with too many women and spent too much money pleasing them with temples to their gods and on other great projects. He bankrupted the nation which was the beginning of its decline, a decline that culminated in the nation's defeat by the Babylonians in 587 B.C. From then on the Jews existed under the subjection of one or another powerful nation.

A couple of hundred years before Christ, there arose a spirit that yearned for freedom and independence and this yearning expressed itself in a number of forms. One such form scholars have named apocalypticism. We can see the word Apocalypse in this word and of course our Apocalypse, or Book of Revelation, is an excellent reflection of apocalyptic thinking. This thinking is reflected in many Jewish writings before and after Jesus. It was also the stimulus for those who rose up in military rebellion against their suppressors. This always brought disaster upon the rebels and usually even on those Jews who did not share in the rebellion. I hasten to add that not all who held an apocalyptic viewpoint engaged in such violence. John the Baptist and Jesus were apocalyptic in their thinking and preaching, but they lived and preached peace. In general the apocalyptic viewpoint was that the world was suffering under the dominion of evil forces. But God would soon overthrow the forces of evil, including especially the enemies of Israel, and establish his good kingdom. Those who lived good lives would enjoy the blessings of the kingdom while those who were evil would be excluded from the kingdom. Moreover, apocalyptic expectations at the time of Jesus were that this new world over which God would reign would come about in a very short time. Knowing something about apocalypticism is a great help in understanding the gospel. I might mention that Mark and Luke always refer to this new world order that God will establish as the kingdom of God. Matthew prefers to call it the kingdom of heaven (so as not to use the word "God" out of deference to God's name and title), but kingdom of heaven and kingdom of God mean the same thing.

Today we hear three more parables about the kingdom. The third about the net full of fish and anything else that got caught in the net is similar to the parable of the wheat and the weeds we heard last week. The kingdom will be made up of saints and sinners until the end of the world as we know it and God's kingdom takes over. The first two about the hidden treasure and the pearl of great value demonstrate the joy that belong to those who have found the kingdom and their willingness to sacrifice all for the sake of the kingdom. Indeed, some have given up everything, including their lives, for the kingdom. However, even if our lives and all our possessions are not required of us, we all have to give up our selfish, self-centered egos in order to have hearts open to love God above all things and to love others as we do ourselves.

I have two quick thoughts before I finish: I think Paul's statement in today's second reading certainly expresses an apocalyptic outlook on life. "We know that all things work for good for those who love God." It is a Scripture verse that I often quote to myself when things get difficult. It helps me to keep a positive attitude and to keep going. Secondly, pearls were highly prized in the ancient world. From Pliny the Elder, an ancient historian, we learn that Cleopatra is said to have possessed a single pearl worth a little more than $4,000,000. What is the kingdom worth to you? Amen.

Eighteenth Sunday in Ordinary Time
July 31, 2011

INTRODUCTION – (Isaiah 55:1-3; Roman 8:35, 37-39; Matthew 14:13-21) Today's first reading is an invitation to the Jews who had been exiled in Babylon for 50 years. Surely by this time very few Jews were still living who had ever seen Jerusalem. Yet those in exile had heard stories about the land they lost and were yearning to return home. The prophet we hear this morning tells them they are free to do so. His message covers 15 chapters in the latter part of the Book of Isaiah. Their liberation was happening through the benevolence of the Persian King, Cyrus, who had been able to conquer the Babylonians. Through King Cyrus, God was fulfilling his promise that he would bring his people back to their own land, a land flowing with milk and honey. They would now find nourishment from their own lands. If the food God provided for them sounds pretty basic: grain, bread, wine, milk, it must have sounded like a lavish banquet to an oppressed people. Our first reading prepares us for the gospel which is also about food.

HOMILY – If you think it's hot here, imagine what it must be like in Texas. Rumor has it that the mosquitoes are flying around with canteens. The farmers are giving crushed ice to their chickens to keep them from laying hard-boiled eggs. A fire hydrant was seen bribing a dog. The Baptists are starting to baptize by sprinkling, the Methodists are using wet-wipes, the Presbyterians are giving out rain-checks and the Catholics are praying for the wine to change back into water.

For the past three weeks, we have heard seven parables about the kingdom of heaven. Jesus didn't just preach about the kingdom, he demonstrated it. He demonstrated it in casting out demons, healing the sick, raising the dead, forgiving sins and in feeding the multitude.

Last week I dedicated a significant portion of my homily to the apocalyptic vision that was current around the time of Jesus. The general notion of apocalypticism was that the world was suffering under the dominion of evil forces. But God would soon overthrow the forces of evil (including, and especially, the enemies of Israel) and establish his good kingdom. Those who lived good lives would enjoy the blessings of the kingdom while those who were evil would be excluded from the kingdom. Moreover, apocalyptic expectations at the time of Jesus were that this new world over which God would reign would come about in a very short time. Knowing something about apocalyptic thinking is a great help in understanding the gospel for preparing ourselves for God's good kingdom is the basic message of Jesus.

We heard the prophet in today's first reading telling God's people, in poetic terms, that God alone can give them what they need. The prophet uses the image of grain and bread, water, wine and milk and rich fare all for free – all they have to do is to come to God and not go away from him as they had done. Going away from God is what led to the exile in the first place. Jesus used a similar image a couple of times when he told about the kingdom: the parable that is probably most familiar is the one that tells us the kingdom is like a king who gave a wedding feast for his son, when many of those invited excused themselves from what would have been a grand event. (The recent royal wedding of William and Kate would perhaps have been comparable to the wedding in Jesus' parable, except that in Jesus' culture, wedding celebrations would go on for a few days). (Matthew 22:2).

So when Jesus fed a great crowd in a miraculous way, it would not be surprising if the people saw this as a sign of God's kingdom and Jesus as the king who would initiate it. St. John tells us as much: "When the people saw the sign he had done, they said, 'This is truly the Prophet, the one who is to come into the world.'" John adds: "Since Jesus knew that they were going to come and carry him off to make him king, he withdrew again to the mountain alone." (John 6:14-15)

There is no doubt that the early Church retold this story of the multiplication of the loaves using Eucharistic language. They saw the Eucharist as God continuing to feed his people with rich food and choice wine – Jesus' own body and blood. Thus the story of the feeding in this deserted place (tradition has it on the shore of the Sea of Galilee) has actions similar to what Jesus did at the Last Supper: he took, he blessed, he broke and he gave the loaves at the miraculous feeding and the bread at the Last Supper.

John the Baptist was Jesus' cousin and most likely his friend. We have hints that Jesus began his ministry as a follower of John the Baptist. The gospel today tells us that when John was put to death, Jesus withdrew by himself. Most likely he needed some time to grieve. But the disciples and the crowd caught up with him. He put his own personal needs aside when he saw the crowd. Matthew and Luke tell us he cured the sick; Mark tells us he taught them. (He probably did both.) As the day began to fade, the issue of food came up. The gospel does not tell us in detail how Jesus achieved this marvelous event, only through faith can we believe that Jesus fed 5000 men (not counting women and children) with five loaves and two fish. The Lord continues to feed us in a miraculous way today – a mysterious feeding that also requires our faith. In the Eucharist today we also have a sign of the coming kingdom, when we will be united with Jesus our Lord and savior forever. Paul confirms this when he tells us in the second reading that, in spite of our unworthiness, nothing in all of creation will separate us from his love. Amen.

Nineteenth Sunday in Ordinary Time
August 7, 2011

INTRODUCTION – (1 Kings 19:9a, 11-13a; Romans 9:1-5; Matthew 14:22-33) Our first reading today takes us back roughly 860 years before Christ. It was the time of Elijah the prophet. Ahaz was king in Israel, but the real power behind the throne was the infamous Queen Jezebel. Jezebel was an impassioned promoter of paganism of the worship of the Canaanite god Baal. Elijah, of course, was just as passionate in trying to keep God's people faithful to the God of Israel. So you might imagine they would clash and they did. Elijah challenged all the prophets of Baal to a contest on Mt. Carmel which ended in Elijah's victory and the annihilation of all the pagan prophets. Certainly Christ would not have handled it the way Elijah did, but

Christ wouldn't be born for another eight and a half centuries. In spite of the obvious outcome of the contest, which proved Israel's God was the true God, Jezebel was furious and vowed blood vengeance on Elijah. To save his life, Elijah fled from Israel to Mt. Horeb in Sinai, the very same place where Moses gave Israel the Ten Commandments and where God made a covenant with Israel. There Elijah heard God's voice, not in dramatic natural phenomena, but in the silence of his heart.

HOMILY – A doctor phoned his patient one afternoon and told him: "I have some bad news and some worse news. The bad news is that all your tests show you have 24 hours to live." The patient said, "What could be worse than that?" The doc answered, "I've been trying to reach you since yesterday."

Pope John Paul II became pope in October, 1978. There was lots of bad news then. The cold war was threatening world peace. Modern culture was destroying traditional social and moral values. Priests and nuns were abandoning their vocations in huge numbers. Conservatives and liberals were battling over the implementation of Vatican II. His message to the Church and the world at the beginning of his long pontificate are the words we hear in today's gospel: "Be not afraid."

Fear, of course, is a healthy thing when it motivates us to protect ourselves from some threat to the wellbeing of ourselves or of those we love. Fear stimulates us emotionally to prepare for fight or flight. But a lot of people are consumed by fears that are groundless, irrational, or certain things we can do nothing about except pray.

In last week's gospel, we heard about Jesus miraculously feeding over 5000 people with five loaves of bread and two fish. Matthew immediately follows that gospel with today's gospel. The miraculous feeding took place on the sea of Galilee. Jesus made the disciples get into a boat and he went off to the hills alone to pray. Matthew leaves us to wonder why Jesus acted this way. St. John fills in some of the details. John tells us that after the crowd had seen what Jesus did in healing the sick and feeding all of them, they decided they were going to make him their king. As king, he would be their liberator and savior. He would raise an army and drive the Romans out of Israel and Judea. He would rule them, maybe even fulfill every need they had. Jesus knew that's not what the Father sent him to do. As savior he had much greater things to offer them than freedom from the powers of Rome and free meals. So Jesus sent the Apostles away because he knew they would be particularly excited over the prospect of Jesus taking over as king. Some of them already imagined themselves having important places in Jesus' kingdom. So he sent them off, away from the crowd, dismissed the crowd himself and went off alone to pray.

The story of Jesus walking on the water is an unusual miracle. Usually when Jesus worked a miracle, he was responding to someone's needs: hunger, sickness, evil spirit possession, storms on the sea. Jesus walking on the water is simply a manifestation of his divine nature. There are numerous references in the Old Testament to God walking on the water or the sea. Seeing him approaching them, the Apostles panicked and Jesus said: "take courage, it is I, be not afraid." "It is I" is an important part of this gospel because it gives greater clarity about what this event meant. It could mean, "it's just me." But it is also in Greek the name that God gave Moses when Moses wanted to know God's name: "I am," or "I am who I am." "ἐγώ εἰμί" All Jews knew this sacred name but no one ever pronounced it except the High Priest once a year in the Holy of Holies. Why does Jesus wish to reveal himself in this way? First of all it is important to note that in all three gospels that tell the story of Jesus walking on water, it immediately follows the story of the miraculous feeding and is linked to it. If you remember last week, the miraculous feeding anticipated the Eucharist in that it tells us Jesus took bread, blessed it, broke it and gave it. These are the same verbs used at the Last Supper in the account of the institution of the Eucharist. The Eucharistic symbolism that begins with the miracle of the feeding continues into the story of walking on the water. There we have the Apostles struggling in the night, with the wind against them, feeling as if they were making no progress. Suddenly Jesus assures them of his presence. He would not desert them. You might recall his words at the Last Supper: "I will not leave you orphans". He brings courage and calms their fears by announcing his presence, which he will also do for us, and which he especially does in the Eucharist when he tells us: "this is my body," "this is my blood."

Matthew joins a story about Peter to his account of Jesus walking on the water. It points out the special position of Peter as do many other passages in the New Testament. It also shows Peter that, with Christ's bidding and with his help, Peter would be able to do amazing things. So can any of us when our Lord invites us to follow him and is there to hold us up. I can't say how many times the presence, especially in the Eucharist, strengthened me and helped me in difficult times. So he is with us now at Mass today telling us as he told the Apostles: "be not afraid." Amen.

20th Sunday in Ordinary Time
August 14, 2011

INTRODUCTION – (Isaiah 56:1, 6-7; Romans 11:13-15, 29-32; Matthew 15:21-28) Our theme is expressed in the psalm refrain: "O God, let all the nations praise you." God wants all nations and all people to know him and love him, and God desires to share his love with all people. We take this for granted. However, the first believers in Christ were Jewish. They insisted that for Gentiles to become believers, they first had to become Jews and be circumcised and follow all the Jewish rituals and customs, fasting obligations, restricted diet and temple sacrifices. We read in the Acts of the Apostles that Peter at first, and then Paul, said, "no way would all that be required – salvation comes through Christ who is the fulfillment of the Law." The Apostles and early Christians insisted that the moral obligations of the law needed to be observed (such as the Ten Commandments), but the fight was over as to whether Gentile Christians had to observe Jewish cultic and ritual laws. Our first reading, a passage from the Book of Isaiah (written 500 years before Christ), foretells that Gentiles (called "foreigners" in the reading) would someday worship in God's Temple and could even offer sacrifices. Even 500 years later, during Jesus' time, Jews were very exclusive as to their special claim on God. For example, there were major divisions as to where people could go when they came to the Temple. The courtyard of the priests was closest to the Temple itself, next closest was the courtyard for Jewish men, then further out was the courtyard for Jewish women, then furthest from the Temple itself was the courtyard of the Gentiles. Gentiles were forbidden by death to go beyond their section. Isaiah, in today's first reading, is proposing an extremely radical concept that Gentiles would offer sacrifice in the Temple. There is even a hint further on in Isaiah that some of the Gentiles would be chosen to be priests and Levites. How this ties in with the gospel I will explain at the end of my homily.

HOMILY – This is a poem that always made me smile. It's entitled Semantics:

Call a woman a kitten, but never a cat;
You can call her a mouse, cannot call her a rat;
Call a woman a chicken, but never a hen;
Or you surely will not be her caller again.
You can call her a duck, cannot call her a goose;
You can call her a deer, but never a moose;
You can call her a lamb, but never a sheep;
Economic she lives, but you can't call her cheap.
You can say she's a vision, can't say she's a sight;
And no woman's skinny, she's slender and slight.
If she should burn you up, say she sets you afire,
And you'll always be welcome, you tricky old liar.

This poem illustrates how two different words, close in meaning, can evoke very different reactions. In today's gospel, Jesus meets a pagan woman, a Greek, living in the neighborhood of Tyre and Sidon. The area itself tells us she was probably a financially well-to-do person. She was a woman who was a loving mother and a very clever person. This is a unique story. I cannot think of any other story where Jesus seems so harsh with someone seeking his help. It's also the only one I can think of where someone got the better of Jesus in a debate. I would guess that the only part of this story that most people remember is Jesus saying to her "it is not right to take the food of the children (the Jews) and throw it to the dogs (meaning Gentiles)." Referring to someone as a dog in those days, as well as today, would be an insult. A dog would be an unclean animal for the Jews, just as Gentiles were considered unclean by the Jews. What if Jesus had said: "it is not right to take the food of the children and throw it to the birds?" Birds were unclean, too, for Jews. Would that have been less offensive? Actually in the Greek, the word that is used here generally means a puppy or a pet, rather than a mangy cur that just freely roamed the neighborhood. Was puppy offensive? I guess we'll never know which word would be most cutting. The important thing to notice is that the woman didn't turn and walk away in a huff. She was humble enough and clever enough and persistent enough to accept Jesus' remark and turn it to her advantage in order to gain his help to heal her daughter.

I have brief comments before I conclude. In the gospel, the healing is not the primary focus of the story. It is the conversation between Jesus and the woman. In that we find a lesson for ourselves. How many times have we prayed earnestly for something, something very dear to us, and God seems to have ignored us or rebuffed us. We turn on our heels and walk away, angry, promising we will quit praying or going to Church or thinking God just doesn't care about me. Jesus has on other occasions in the gospels insisted on the importance of perseverance in prayer and not giving up. The woman in the gospel wouldn't give up.

A second point goes back to what I said in my introduction, to the issue the early Church was dealing with about the conversion of the Gentiles (do they have to become Jews before they could become Christians). Fortunately the issue was settled long ago and we don't have to deal with it. But surely this story of the Canaanite woman would have been on the minds of those who lived during the first century after Jesus. It's most likely this is precisely why the evangelists recorded the event. The story shows that although Jesus' mission was not to the Gentiles before he was crucified, he was not opposed to their having a full share in God's love and blessings. If the early Church had decided Gentiles must first become Jews in order to share in God's kingdom, the gospel probably would not have spread as widely and as rapidly as it did. Thus, we might never have come to know about Jesus except as some obscure person in history. And so, every Sunday, as we do today, we come together to hear about Jesus and to celebrate the love God has for us and for all people. Amen.

Feast of the Assumption
August 14/15, 2000

INTRODUCTION AT THE VIGIL – (1 Chr 15:3-4, 15-16; 16:1-2; 1 Cor 15:5b-57; Luke 11:27-28) It is a dogma of our faith that at the end of her life, Mary, like her son, was taken body and soul into heaven. This is the meaning of the Assumption, whose vigil we celebrate this evening.

Our first reading is about the Ark of the Covenant, the sacred gold plated box that contained the Ten Commandments and on top of which were two golden angels (similar to the two angels on our tabernacle doors if you can see them.) The Ark was the unique symbol of God's presence with Israel. It was constructed in the desert after Moses and the Israelites left Egypt. It led them into the Promised Land. Often it was taken into battle with them. When King David established his capital in Jerusalem about the year 1000 BC, he brought the Ark there. Today's reading describes this solemn and joyful occasion. After the temple was built, the Ark was placed in the Holy of Holies and there it remained for 400 years until the Babylonians destroyed the temple.

In Christian symbolism, Mary is sometimes referred to as the Ark of the Covenant. As the Ark represented the special presence of God dwelling with his people, Mary carried within herself Jesus who is truly Son of God dwelling with us.

MASS DURING THE DAY – (Rev 11:19a; 12:1-6a, 10ab; 1 Cor 15:20-27; Luke 1: 39-56) It is a dogma of our faith that at the end of her life, Mary, like her son, was taken body and soul into heaven. This is the meaning of the Assumption, the feast we celebrate today.

In our first reading from Revelation, we hear about a woman, a child and a dragon. The dragon is the devil and the powers of evil at work in the world. The child is Christ. The woman in our reading has a double symbolism. She stands for Mary, the physical mother of Jesus Christ and she stands for the Church, our spiritual mother who brings Jesus Christ to birth in us through faith and the sacraments. The glorious way in which the woman is described has a double symbolism too. It symbolizes the glory of Mary in the assumption and it also symbolizes the glory which we, the faithful, the Church, hope to enjoy one day.

HOMILY – St. Francis de Sales asks the simple question in his sermon for the Assumption: "What son would not bring his mother back to life and would not bring her into paradise after her death if he could?" Who could argue with a statement like that? In Mary's Assumption the glory of Jesus' resurrection is first of all extended to his mother, but as we celebrate it we celebrate likewise our own hope to share in this risen glory some day. We recite this belief in the last lines of the creed: "We believe in the resurrection of the dead, and the life of the world to come."

It's interesting that the Holy Father declared the dogma of the Assumption during a difficult time in recent history. In 1950, when the doctrine of the Assumption was declared by Pope Pius XII, we had experienced two world wars, the Holocaust, the Atomic Bomb and the beginning of the Cold War. The world had enough reason to feel hopeless. Contrasted with the pessimism of the time, this dogma offers hope, hope that the destiny of the human race is more than wars, destruction and devastation. At about that same time in 1950, the cult of the body and the glories of sexuality were beginning to take hold of society. The Church leaders could see that the more that sex and the body were idolized the more society would lose its respect for marriage and family values. In contrast to the glorification of the body as an object of pleasure, this dogma affirms the true dignity and the beauty of the body and the source of that dignity and beauty which is God's grace within us.

In the Assumption Mary is fully united with her son in glory. She remains his mother. He remains her son. Cardinal Suenens once said, "Jesus does not point out Mary and say, 'She used to be my mother.'" Not only is she Jesus' mother, she is our mother too, for on Calvary Jesus gave her to us to be our mother. "Woman, behold your son," he said to her and to St. John, who was a representative of all disciples, Jesus said "Behold your mother." We know and believe that Mary is concerned about our salvation. We expect Mary to help us and we pray to her. Protestants sometimes have trouble with this idea of praying to Mary. Jesus is our savior and we all believe that. But Protestants believe we should pray for one another. If we can ask others to pray for us and we pray for them, why can't those in heaven also pray for us? Are we now so separated from those who have died so that they no longer can help us or be concerned about us? If we seek the prayers of sinners on earth, for we are all sinners, why not seek the intercession of the saints in heaven? Why not turn to the Queen of saints, God's own Mother?

The Assumption tells us that God is not only concerned about our souls but also about our bodies. They are temples of the Spirit. They are part of who we are, and so the feast of the Assumption is a feast that celebrates who we shall be.

In addition to the Arc of the Covenant being a symbol for Mary, there is an another way in which today's first reading connects with today's feast. In Christian literature, especially in the book of Revelation, Jerusalem symbolizes our heavenly home. Thus, the Ark being taken to Jerusalem symbolized Mary being taken body and soul into the heavenly kingdom.

21st Sunday in Ordinary Time
August 24, 2008

INTRODUCTION – (Isaiah 22:19-23, Romans 11: 33-36, Matthew 16:13-20) Shebna was a powerful man in the court of King Hezekiah in Judah, 700 years before Christ. Next to the king, he had the most powerful position in the kingdom. Shebna's power went to his head and he used his position to exploit the poor and the innocent in order to make himself exorbitantly rich. God said through Isaiah that Shebna needed to be replaced by a person with integrity. The only reason this passage was selected for today's reading was because of the reference to the key of the House of David. Keys are symbols of authority. In our gospel Jesus promises he would give Peter the keys to the kingdom of heaven.

HOMILY – I want to make a point about something I saw in the Enquirer this past week, then I want to reflect on two important ideas in today's gospel.

There was a brief news clip in Thursday's paper about a hacker who broke into the telephone system of FEMA last weekend and racked up about $12,000 in long distance phone calls to the Middle East and Asia. FEMA is part of Homeland Security. I didn't feel real secure after reading that! If this isn't a good incentive for people to pray for our country and our world, I don't know what is. Psalm 127 says: "If the Lord does not build the house, in vain do its builders labor; if the Lord does not watch over the city, in vain does the watchman keep vigil." We live in a society that keeps us so busy that often prayer is relegated to "something I'll do when I have the time." We are constantly being told our government is doing a great job of protecting us and I can only assume they are doing the best they can, but can we depend totally on the government? When was the last time we actually asked God to help our country. You might say a hacker breaking into a department of Homeland Security phone system and charging $12,000 in long distance phone calls is just a small thing, and maybe it is, but wars have been won and lost over seemingly small things. I say all this, not with the intent of frightening people, but with the intent of reminding all of us we need to constantly pray. "If the Lord does not watch over the city, in vain does the watchman keep vigil."

Now I want to reflect on two important ideas in today's gospel. First of all there are many places in the Scriptures that emphasize the preeminent position of Peter among the apostles, but there are two places where Peter's position of leadership is spelled out more clearly than anywhere else. The one is in St. John where Jesus tells Peter after the resurrection: "Feed my lambs, feed my sheep." Also in Scripture where Peter's position of importance is clearly emphasized is in today's gospel. Such insistence on the position of Peter vis-à-vis the other apostles is what underlies our belief that after Christ, the Holy Father is chief shepherd and head of the Church. His role is to be the visible representative of Christ. This doesn't mean he has perfectly represented Christ at all times in history, but that is still the position he holds. He has the final word on any issue relating to the Church. The keys Jesus said he would give Peter symbolize this authority. The keys Jesus gave Peter were not buried with him and that position of authority did not end when Peter died. It was passed on to his successors. This is implied in the gospel Matthew wrote, for Peter had been dead for at least 25 or 30 years when Matthew wrote this passage. Matthew made a big issue of this incident, not to tell us about some personal favor Jesus bestowed on Peter, but because the leadership position of Peter would remain as part of the structure of Christ's community of believers.

A second important idea in today's gospel is the answer to the question Jesus asked his apostles: "Who do you say that I am?" How we answer this question will determine how each of us relates to him. Is he, for example, someone worth our time on Sunday or even during the week? Is he someone we can trust? Is he someone who loves us, forgives us, wants only the best for us? Is he someone who has the authority to tell us how to live, what we should do, what we may not do? Is he someone we look forward to spending eternity with?

Can any of us give a complete and perfect answer to that question "Who do you say that I am?" In one way or another, each week I try to help you have a better sense of how to answer this question, even as I try to answer it for myself. It's easy to say Jesus is savior, Jesus is messiah,

Jesus is Son of God, or as we say in the creed each week: Jesus is "God from God, light from light, true God from true God, etc." But has our mind and heart connected with these words to the extent that we can exclaim with Paul: "Oh, the depth of the riches and wisdom and knowledge of God! ... For from him and through him and for him are all things." The apostles could tell Jesus what others said about him, and we can also say what others have said about Jesus. That's okay, for that's how we begin to learn who Jesus is, by what others tell us. But have we moved beyond what others have told us to know Jesus in a personal way, a way that Jesus could say has not been revealed to us by "flesh and blood, but by the Heavenly Father?" If we do not know Jesus personally, what can we do that will help us to know him, not just by hearsay, but in a deeply personal way? How we do it is how we get to know anyone in a personal way. By spending time with a person. There are no shortcuts. Spending time with God, with Jesus, is called prayer. That's what we are about now. Amen.

22nd Sunday in Ordinary Time
August 28, 2011

INTRODUCTION – (Jeremiah 20:7-9) Our first reading from the prophet Jeremiah goes back to 600 B.C. It sounds as if Jeremiah thought that when God called him to be a prophet, it would be an easy job. But the people who heard God's message only hated Jeremiah for what he preached. They ridiculed him, threw him in jail and even tried to kill him. We hear him complaining to God, "You duped me! You tricked me, God!"

Jesus' faithfulness to his mission would bring him suffering too, but Jesus did not complain or feel duped.

He was well aware of what was going to happen. In today's gospel, we hear him warning his disciples ahead of time.

HOMILY – (Matthew 16:21-27) I don't know where I saw this and I'm not sure who said it, but some wit said: "If anyone should doubt whether this is truly the land of promise, they should show up around election time." Politicians promise all the good things they will do for us. You would never hear a politician say, like Jesus did in today's gospel, "Whoever wishes to come after me must deny himself, take up his cross and follow me."

Most of us are like Peter in today's reading. We are happy to hear about the peace, love and joy that our faith can bring us, and it can, but we don't want to hear about the cross. If you remember last Sunday's gospel, Jesus asks the Apostles, "Who do you say that I am?" Peter makes a profound act of faith when he says, "You are the Christ (the Messiah, the Savior). You are the Son of the living God." Then Jesus told the Apostles what being the messiah would involve. He would suffer greatly, be killed and on the third day be raised. Peter objected. He didn't want to hear any of that negative stuff. Jesus refused to back down from Peter's objections. On the contrary, Jesus predicted suffering for his followers too, "whoever wishes to come after me must deny himself, take up his cross and follow me."

Jesus used some of the strongest language in rebuking Peter that we hear anywhere in the gospels: "Get behind me, Satan." He wasn't saying Peter was an evil person, he was saying Peter was doing the work of Satan, being a tempter, trying to talk Jesus out of his mission, part of which involved rejection and suffering. Jesus knew the Scriptures and the history of God's people better than Peter and he knew what happened to prophets whose mission was to preach God's word, such as Jeremiah whom we hear in the first reading and John the Baptist, Jesus' cousin, who had just been beheaded by Herod. We cannot be too critical of Peter, however, for we have the advantage of hindsight and we know that what Jesus went through had a happy ending with the resurrection. Jesus' being raised on the third day would have been beyond Peter's ability to comprehend. It would have been too much for us to understand, too, if we had been there.

Jesus said "whoever wishes to come after me must deny himself, take up his cross and follow me." It's a wonder that anyone decided to follow Jesus when he talked like that. The cross, whether it was a wooden one as it was for Jesus, or some other form of martyrdom, has been real for many of Christ's followers throughout the centuries. For those like us who are not in immediate danger of being persecuted for our faith, carrying the cross involved the day to day effort to overcome our selfishness and to love God with our whole heart and soul, mind and strength and to love our neighbor as ourselves. The cross is for most of us, as St. Paul says in today's second reading, (Romans 12:1-2) "offering ourselves as a living sacrifice, holy and pleasing to God."

Jesus came to establish God's kingdom, a kingdom where God would "wipe away every tear from our eyes, where there would be no more death or mourning, wailing or pain" (Revelation 21:4). Jesus didn't come to us to tell us it is good to have to suffer, he came to bring us a better world; he healed the sick, he drove out demons, he told people to help the poor. Suffering for its own sake is never any good. It's a reasonable thing to do what we can to try to alleviate it. But there are some crosses, some sufferings we cannot avoid. They are part of our journey to God. There are also those crosses we may have to bear that are part of our responsibility or our vocation of caring for others, crosses that sometimes parents have to endure, or religious or missionaries or adult children of aged parents, or they are the crosses that are part of our jobs like teachers or firemen or service men and women or whatever; those are the crosses that bring us closer to our Lord who carried a cross for us.

When we come to Mass we recall Jesus' love for us and the sacrifice he made for us. It is especially here that he gives us the strength to follow him and to offer ourselves as a living sacrifice, holy and pleasing to God, our spiritual worship. Amen.

23rd Sunday in Ordinary Time
September 4, 2011

INTRODUCTION – (Ezekiel 33:7-9; Romans 13:8-10; Matthew 18:15-20) Our first reading takes us back six hundred years before Christ as God explains to his prophet Ezekiel his responsibility as a prophet. Ezekiel must warn God's people of their sinful ways or he will be held accountable. It is a prelude to the gospel where Jesus instructs his followers how to help each other stay on the right track. St. Paul's teaching on love in our second reading reminds us that if we should try to correct one another, it should be done out of love.

HOMILY – There was an 85 year-old lady who found her husband in bed with another woman. She was so enraged that she dragged him to the balcony of their Miami high-rise and pushed him off, and he fell to his death. She was arrested, of course, and when she appeared before the judge he asked if she had anything to say in her own defense. "Well, your honor," she said, "I figured if he were able to be unfaithful to his wife at age 92, he surely would be able to fly." (*Reader's Digest*,

Laughter, the Best Medicine, pg 365)

We've all had times when we were angry enough to throw someone off a high building, but that's not the way Jesus tells us to deal with the sin of another person. St. Matthew's gospel contains five large sections of Jesus' teachings that are called "major discourses." We are all familiar with the first major discourse we call "the Sermon on the Mount." Our gospel today is taken from the fourth major discourse called the Social Discourse where he teaches us how he expects his followers to treat others. Our gospel introduces one of the topics Jesus spoke on in the Social Discourse with these words: "If your brother sins against you ..." Two of the oldest and best Greek manuscripts do not have the words "against you." They say simply "if your brother sins" period. Most commentators hold that the words "against you" were not part of the original gospel. Thus our topic today is how to deal with a person who has committed or is committing some sin. Jesus outlines a three-step process: 1) talk with the person personally to win them over; i.e., to sway them to give up their wrongdoing; if that approach fails 2) confront the person in the presence of two or three witnesses and 3) bring the person before the whole Church. As a last step, if the person does not repent, they are to be excluded from the community; i.e., they are excommunicated. At issue here is obviously a sin of a serious and public nature. One wouldn't go through this process if it were over some small issue.

Excommunication is a process that is very rare today; It is applied only for the most serious sins. Examples of such sins would be: abortion, a priest breaking the seal of confession, a person trying to say Mass who is not ordained, physically attacking the Holy Father. These are serious sins that can be very destructive to a community – like a deadly contagious disease. The process is meant to give the offender every opportunity to repent of their sinful ways. Although excommunication is reserved for the most serious offenses, today's topic does have a meaning for a majority of us here. I have spoken with many parents or grandparents who are distressed over the kind of life their children or grandchildren are living and they don't know what to do about it. Today's gospel encourages all of us to do what we can to lead another, who is straying from God's ways, back to our Lord. This is a very sensitive, challenging and difficult thing to do. It must always be done in love. In my efforts at times to do this, I think many of those who received my encouragement to turn over a new leaf recognized I was doing it for their best interest, and I was. In all truthfulness, I was also mindful of God's warning to Ezekiel in today's first reading: if "you do not speak out to dissuade the wicked from his way, the wicked shall die for his guilt, but I will hold you responsible for his death." Those are strong words. I know that in the old days, when I was growing up, priests were often very stern and sometimes harsh and their attitude drove a lot of people away from Church. I know that's why I held back from saying what I should have said at times. I'm sure that I will have some accounting to do for times I didn't speak out. In reminding a person of their religious obligations, I'm not proposing I am holier than anyone else. God will judge that. I just try to do what I think our Lord wants. I usually encourage other people to do that too – to just try.

It isn't easy to do, trying to live holy lives, because we have our culture working against us. However, Christianity has often had to be counter-cultural. In the early centuries people were put to death because they were Christians. Now we are free to practice our faith, and while many people believe in God or in Christ, practicing that faith is not always a high priority in today's world.

I guess I'm preaching to the choir here, because if practicing your faith isn't important to you, you wouldn't be here. So thank you for coming.

When I was a young priest, I was going to convert the world. I found out converting just one person is often a challenge. People don't like to change if they are comfortable with their way of life. Don't get discouraged if you try to lead someone away from doing something that is harming them. If your efforts fall on deaf ears, there is always prayer, which Jesus reminds us of at the end of today's gospel. Prayer is something we can and should always do for those we care about and want to help. I will end with the same words St. James used to end his letter: "whoever brings back a sinner from the error of his way will save his (or her) soul from death and will cover a multitude of sins." (James 5:20) Amen.

Feast of the Holy Cross
September 14, 2008

INTRODUCTION – (Numbers 21: 4b-9, Philippians 2:6-11, John 3:13-17) Our first reading takes us back over a thousand years before Christ, to the time when Moses was leading God's people from slavery in Egypt to the freedom of the Promised Land. The trip through the desert was extremely difficult and at times the people complained bitterly. One of their difficulties was an encounter with a nest of poisonous serpents whose bite brought intense suffering and burning pain and then death. The serpents were called saraph serpents, for saraph means "fiery." The people saw this as punishment for their complaining. But God gave them a way to be healed from the serpent's bite.

The remedy might remind us of the symbol often used today as an icon of the medical profession. In today's gospel, Jesus compares this event to his crucifixion.

HOMILY – During Holy Week we focus on the sufferings of Christ crucified. Today our focus is more on the glory and victory of the cross. In Jesus' day the cross was an instrument of torture, brutality and shame. The Romans reserved it for the worse criminals and enemies of the Roman Empire. If a criminal was a Roman citizen, he or she was exempt from crucifixion because it was such a terrible way to die. Roman citizens were simply beheaded. But Jesus has turned the cross into a symbol of victory, a symbol of hope, a symbol of sacrifice and infinite love. St. Paul tells us in Galatians (2:20) "I live by faith in the Son of God who has loved me and given himself up for me."

Over and over the Scriptures tell us through the cross Jesus saved us, but early Christian art seldom pictured the cross. They didn't need to. Father Foley in Saint of the Day said: "It stood outside too many city walls, decorated only with decaying corpses, as a threat to anyone who defied Rome's authority." Included in this group of those who defied Rome's authority were the Christians who would not worship pagan gods, but only the Father, the Lord Jesus and the Spirit. The emperor Constantine who made Christianity legal in 313 also eliminated crucifixion as a form of capital punishment. Once the Roman Empire actually ceased crucifying people, then images of the cross appeared in Christian art. These first images of the cross did not include an image of the suffering Christ, but they were crosses decorated with jewels and precious metals. Incidentally it was a vision of the cross that led to the conversion of Constantine. He was assured in the vision that in the sign of the cross he would conquer Maxentius, a rival to the throne, and he would become emperor of Rome.

Once Constantine gained control of the Roman Empire, he went to the Holy Land with his mother, St. Helen, to discover the places where Jesus lived and died. Constantine and his mother had churches built in Bethlehem and the Mount of Olives but the most famous church he built is the Church of the Holy Sepulcher, built over the hill of Calvary and the tomb of Jesus. It was in the process of building the Church of the Holy Sepulcher that Jesus' cross was found. How did they know it was Jesus' cross? Legend has it that the men working on this project found three crosses and they didn't know which one was Jesus' cross. They touched each of the crosses to a woman who was dying and when she was touched with the third cross, she was instantly healed. Today's feast of the Holy Cross goes back to that time, around the year 320 AD. It celebrates the finding of the true cross and the dedication of the Basilica of the Holy Sepulcher. So that's why this feast is celebrated in the middle of September and not during Lent as we might expect.

Today's gospel is sometimes called the gospel in miniature. These few verses express the essence of the entire gospel: God's offer of eternal life through the sacrifice of Christ, a sacrifice offered out of love for us. God so loved the world, God so loved you and me that he gave us the greatest gift, the gift of his son, so we would know the greatest blessing: eternal happiness with him.

Today we approach the cross not with sorrow but with joy, not as a symbol of death but of life, not as a sign of defeat but of victory, not as a cause for fear but of hope, not as an instrument of cruelty and hatred but of eternal love. On a practical level, I know somehow it was inevitable if Jesus were to be true to his mission. If he had run away from it, he would not have risen and his message would have soon been forgotten. Today Christians make up one third of the world's population. If Jesus had abandoned his mission to change the world through love, perhaps some obscure history book might have had a sentence or two about this person who did a lot of healing and was a good preacher, but for the most part his ministry would be forgotten. This is just a superficial explanation of the mystery of the cross. There is much more to this mystery, but each of us has to discover it for ourselves. To come to a deeper understanding takes lots of prayer – and that's what the Mass does for us each week, it reminds us of God's love and the hope and joy and freedom and peace and salvation it gives us. Amen.

25th Sunday in Ordinary Time
September 18, 2011

INTRODUCTION – (Isaiah 25: 6-9; Mt. 20: 1-16) When God's people were in exile in Babylon, they were as depressed as anyone could possibly be. They had lost everything. They were sure they had even lost God's love because of their sinfulness. Today we hear God's prophet assure them it is never too late to return to the Lord. Even though they knew they were not worthy of it, they will have God's mercy if they will reform their lives. God is forgiving, not because we are worthy, but because it is God's nature to be generous and forgiving. The theme of God's generosity prepares us for today's gospel.

HOMILY – Jesus' parables, as always, are designed to shock us into thinking. It's normal for us to feel the employer was unfair and that's exactly how Jesus knew we would feel. It is true, the owner was more generous with some than with others, but was he unfair with anyone?

In Jesus' society a laborer was paid at the end of the day and the normal pay was just enough for a person to feed his family for one day. Could it be that the owner of the vineyard was more generous with some so that none of the people who worked for him that day would have to beg, borrow or steal in order to feed their families the next day? Would that be unfair for the employer to do that? What do you think Jesus was trying to tell us?

The clue to understanding the parable is the first line where Jesus tells us this is what the kingdom of heaven is like. Jesus was telling us why he was always willing to reach out to sinners, something he was frequently criticized for doing. He wants us to know it's never too late to find God if we wish to. Remember the good thief whom Jesus forgave on the cross. If we've not been living right, though, does that mean we can wait until the last minute to straighten ourselves out? If we do we'll miss out on the joy of knowing God's love and presence in our lives right now and who knows whether we'll get the opportunity to repent at the last minute. I think it was St. Augustine who prayed: "God, make me good, but not right now!" Not a good prayer. Fortunately God paid attention only to the first part of the prayer (God, make me good), and the Church was greatly blessed because God led Augustine from his wayward life to a life of holiness. "The usual daily wage" in the parable is a symbol for the immense happiness we will all have in God's kingdom. Some individuals may be closer to God because they served and loved God more faithfully than others, but we will all be equal in one way, whether we receive God's grace early or late in life, we will all be as happy as we can possibly be.

Jesus explained his forgiveness of sinners by this parable. St. Matthew found it helpful to use this same parable for a similar purpose when he wrote his gospel probably 50 or 60 years after Jesus preached it. During this period, many Jewish Christians, who had lived their whole lives faithful to God's law, had difficulty accepting new converts into the Church, converts coming from paganism, who represented those who came late to the vineyard. The parable was meant to help Jewish Christians welcome those who came to know Christ later in life and accept them as equals in God's kingdom.

Today we have no problem with these ideas. We are always happy to see people turn their lives toward God, whether they had strayed away at some time in their lives and came back, or whether for the first time, even late in life, they become believers in Christ and join his Church. But there may be a couple of ideas that are relevant for us today. First of all, the people who worked all day complained about unfair treatment. Is Jesus telling us we shouldn't complain when we feel we've been treated unfairly? Well, sometimes complaining is good. It sometimes helps get things done, it helps us get things off our chest, it may help us clarify our thoughts and come to realize we haven't been treated too badly after all. If people didn't complain, counselors and psychologists and doctors would not be able to help people. Politicians wouldn't have anything to do. Friends and family members wouldn't be able to give support and sympathy to each other if they didn't know how their friend or family member hurt. Complaining can be positive, but we have to be careful not to make it a way of life. If we want to complain, it helps to stop and count our blessings and we might realize God has treated us far better than any of us deserve!

The other idea today's parable connects with is envy. Envy makes us miserable. Envy is when we look around at others and think they have much more than we do, they have had more breaks in life than we have, etc. We feel life is not fair and we are depressed over it. I believe God is more than fair with all of us. If we want to compare ourselves with others, we need to compare ourselves also with those who have not been as blessed as we have. Always wanting more may motivate us to achieve in life, but it can also be a formula for constant unhappiness. We need to always focus on the positive, on our blessings and give thanks. I always preach that the key to joy in life is gratitude. God's ways are not our ways, Isaiah tells us. Part of the joy of eternity will be praising God for his abundant love and goodness to us. The "Eucharist" which we pray now, a word which means "thanksgiving," is the most perfect way to do that. Amen.

26th Sunday in Ordinary Time
September 25, 2011

INTRODUCTION – (Ezekiel 18:25-28; Matthew 21:28-32) In 587 B.C. when the Babylonians conquered the Jews, destroyed their cities and Temple, and took the surviving Jews to Babylon as captives and slaves, the Jews concluded God was punishing them for the sins of their ancestors. They complained that God was not being fair to them. In our first reading we hear God tell them, through his prophet Ezekiel, it is their own sins that created the disaster they were suffering. Yet with God the situation is never hopeless. They can always change their ways. We hear a similar message in today's gospel. If we have damaged our relationship with God, we can always change our ways.

HOMILY – John told the funeral director to spare no expense for his father's funeral, so when he received a bill for $10,000, he immediately paid it. The next month John got another bill from the funeral home for

$85 and he figured it was something the funeral director forgot to charge for, so he paid that one. The month after that John got one more bill for $85 and he called the funeral director to ask what this is all about. The director said, "you told me to provide the best funeral we could arrange, so I rented a tuxedo for your father."

A teacher asked a little boy in school, "if you had five dollars and you asked your father for another five dollars, how many dollars would you have?" The boy answered, "five dollars." The teacher shook her head and said, "you don't know your math." The child said, "you don't know my father."

You've been hearing about money for two weeks now and I want to thank all of you for your patience. We are finishing up a professionally organized fund raising program in which all parishes in the Archdiocese are to participate. The Archdiocese purchased the program at a good price because of the high number of parishes participating. This is the last sermon about money you will hear at St. Boniface this year. Although you may get a letter or two. Most parishes have already concluded this successfully. I chose to wait until late this year, so I could see how our finances were doing. This turned out to be a good time for us to participate in this program.

It's been almost twenty years that I've been here. When I helped merge St. Patrick and St. Boniface, St. Boniface was hardly surviving financially. St. Patrick Church had some money to bring with it and with that money and money from the sale of St. Patrick Church and the help of a number of bequests over the years, St. Boniface was able to build up a fairly healthy savings account. Your support of St. Boniface has shown itself in the twenty years of my pastorate in that I've only had to preach on money once a year There were several years when I didn't give a money talk at all. I simply said, "keep doing what you're doing." (So if anyone tells you all they ever talk about is money at St. Boniface, you can assume they haven't been here for Mass very often). We've never had a professionally organized program here in my time. But this program is very timely for us right now. The financial world changed in 2008. For the past three fiscal years, we have come out in the red and have had to dig into our savings: about $60,000 the first time, about $10,000 the second time and this past fiscal year which ended June 30, 2011, we take from our savings almost $9000. Two years ago I started giving back half my salary. Not to brag, but I want people to know that if I ask you to sacrifice I would also be willing to do so. Many of you have responded generously to my past appeals and we are doing better. We've had a couple of windfall donations from bequests recently which put us off to a good start this year. If we do well, we may be able to put back some of it into our savings.

Our efforts to increase our contributions are primarily in order to be able to pay our bills every week, and we get a lot of them. As you will see in the bulletin, our budget for this year has taken a big jump from last year – due to the fact that we kept it extra low last year in expectation of a bequest which did not come through. I know these are hard times for many people and no one knows when things will start to look up. So right now we need an increase in our contributions just to keep doing the things we are doing to serve God's people here. Two weeks ago, Carol Roosa spoke of some possible renovations in our church sanctuary. If the funds are there maybe we can do that, but right now our basic need is just to meet our annual budget for the next year.

Regarding the renovations you heard about, we are many months away from doing anything. That whole idea started with a desire to clean the sanctuary in preparation for the celebration of our 150 anniversary. The ceiling is pretty dirty from candle smoke; some of the angels, especially the ones on top, are damaged from water damage. We called in companies for an estimate on cleaning and pretty much got an answer that cleaning was not possible; that the paint and plaster in many places had deteriorated. It's been fifty years since it's been painted. To paint any part of the church would probably not cost much more than to clean it because of the cost for scaffolding and workers. Cleaning the gold ceiling is especially complicated. I know you want to keep your church beautiful, and I do not think there is a more beautiful church in the archdiocese. Although we would like to do something to make our church look fresher and cleaner, and I don't know what that will be yet, the help we ask for now is not primarily for a renovation (as it seems some people thought), but we're just asking for the help to keep doing what we're doing. You might like to know, our school is holding its own. We have many children on vouchers and we receive a lot of help from CISE. We have five Mercy sisters involved in the school, which is a tremendous help. All the staff is doing a fantastic job of teaching our children (over 200 of them, the most we've had since I've been here).

As I said in my letter to you this week, this is commitment Sunday. I am asking if you will tell us what you are willing to give to St. Boniface each week. In a few moments I will sit down to give the ushers time to pass out the commitment envelopes and to let you fill them out. You will get a thank you letter after you turn it in. If you do not turn it in, I will write to ask if you would consider doing so (even if you can't increase what you're giving). This is not a legal document. We will not badger you if things change for you and you can no longer give what you feel you can right now. But don't be like the son in today's gospel who gave his father the answer the father wanted to hear, but never did anything at all. Knowing what people intend to give helps with knowing how to budget. When the collection is taken up, just put your envelope in the basket with your contribution. If you're doing all you can, and many are, I thank you. If you can increase what you are now giving, I thank you too. I am often touched, when I sign those letters I send every four months, by how generous some of our people are. The Lord will not let you outdo him in generosity. Check off if you do not have contribution envelopes and would like to receive them. And check off if you are interested in electronic giving. I find that is most convenient for me. I will now sit down so the ushers can pass out the pledge envelopes and you can fill them out. Again I thank you for your patience and for your generous help each week. Amen.

27th Sunday in Ordinary Time
October 2, 2011

INTRODUCTION – (Isaiah 5:1-7; Matthew 21:33-43) Most of us know how much work is involved in caring for a garden. Just imagine how much work is involved with setting up an entire vineyard, which is a full time business. Isaiah describes some of what was involved in today's first reading. If we wonder why there needed to be a watchtower in the vineyard, it was needed, both day and night, to protect the grapes from thieves and predators, especially during harvest time. Apparently Isaiah was a musician as well as a talented poet. As he sang his song, we can imagine the shock his audience felt when they discovered they were the vineyard he was singing about. From history we know Isaiah's prophecy literally came to be true when it was first the Assyrians then later the Babylonians who invaded the land of Israel and most of the land was laid waste.

HOMILY – When the lieutenant thought he was calling the mess hall, a sleepy voice answered, "Yeah, whaddaya want?" The lieutenant, a bit pompous, replied, "that's no way to answer the phone when an officer calls," he snarled. "Now let's start over. Pretend I just called you." "Ok." The voice on the other end replied, "Captain's cabin. Captain speaking." Sometimes we think we're pretty much of a big wheel, until someone else takes us down a few notches.

In our gospel that's what Isaiah and Jesus did as they told their stories. Their listeners thought they were big wheels, the most important people in the world, because they were the leaders of God's people (who are represented in both stories as a vineyard). Isaiah and Jesus reminded them they were working for God and God was the one in charge. God judged they were incompetent leaders and were doing great spiritual harm to God's people.

I commented earlier on Isaiah, so I want to focus primarily on Jesus' teaching in the gospel. As Matthew tells us, at the beginning Jesus was talking to the chief priests and elders of the people. These were not his friends. These are the ones who would arrest him, judge him, accuse him before Pilate and get him executed. Jewish leaders in the past had abused, ignored, and even killed many prophets. Now the leaders in Jesus' day would kill the son of the owner of the vineyard (who is God) whom God sent to them. Did you notice this little detail in the story that they would throw the son out of the vineyard and kill him – a reference to Jesus being taken outside the city of Jerusalem to be crucified. Jesus warns them they would soon find themselves no longer in charge and others would be given the responsibility of leading God's people and teaching them the ways of holiness. Holiness is the "fruit" that the owner of the vineyard (God) expected as a return from the workers in the vineyard.

I do not want to make this too complicated, but there are two thoughts I would like to add to the story. I want to point out that last summer I devoted a couple of homilies to the concept of apocalypticism. In general the apocalyptic viewpoint was that the world is under the control of evil forces. But God will soon overthrow the forces of evil, including especially the enemies of Israel, and establish his good kingdom (a kingdom of peace, love, justice and joy). Those who have lived good lives will enjoy the blessings of the kingdom while those people who have been evil would be excluded from the kingdom. Moreover, apocalyptic expectations at the time of Jesus were that this new world over which God would reign would come about in a very short time. Knowing something about apocalypticism is a great help in understanding many of Jesus' teachings. Today's gospel gives us another example of Jesus' apocalyptic message. The kingdom of God would be taken away from the leaders in his own day (leaders who were too big to fail and too important to be put down they thought) and leadership would be given to those who would help God's kingdom (God's people) to produce fruit of holiness for the kingdom.

I see an echo of the story of Adam and Eve in today's gospel. The workers in the vineyard did not want to recognize the owner of the vineyard as being in charge and they lost what they had. Adam and Eve did not want to recognize God as being in charge. They wanted to be in charge and make up their own rules and they lost the paradise, which God had given them. Amen.

28th Sunday Ordinary Time
October 9, 2011

INTRODUCTION – (Isaiah 25:6-10a; Matthew 22: 1-14) Today's first reading and today's gospel give us a beautiful picture of what it is we're praying for when we say "thy will be done." God's will is for our complete and eternal happiness. Our gospel warns us, however, that in order to be part of his beautiful plan, we need to respond to the invitation he offers us.

Our second reading is part of a thank you note St. Paul wrote to the Philippians for the money they sent him to help him most probably while he was in prison. The Philippian community was the only community that were thoughtful enough to offer him any support in his ministry. Responding to the invitation God gave him to serve as an apostle was a difficult job for Paul.

HOMILY – Heaven is going to surpass all our hopes and expectations. It's going to be more wonderful than we can imagine. Because there will be love and joy and peace like we've never experienced, it's hard for God to tell us about it. All he can do is to use images that we are familiar with: a great banquet, a wedding feast, the elimination of suffering and death, wealth that cannot be exhausted as in the hidden treasure, the pearl of great price or the mansion God is preparing for us. Today we heard Isaiah compare it to a great banquet and Jesus compare it to a wedding celebration for a prince which would be an event people would remember for years.

As Jesus tells us, to have all this wonder and joy we must respond to an invitation. We must be wise enough not to turn it down. How will we recognize the invitation when it comes? As I reflected on this week's gospel, I came up with a long list of ways we might recognize it. I won't bore you with everything on my list but just give you a few ideas of how we might recognize it. It sounds something like this: "Come to me all you who labor and are burdened and I will refresh you." Or "I am the good shepherd," a shepherd whose sheep hear his voice and follow him. We hear the invitation in the sermon on the mount when Jesus tells us: "Everyone who listens to these words of mine and acts on them will be like a wise man who built his house on rock." Or from the Book of Revelation: "Behold I stand at the door and knock. If anyone hears my voice and opens the door, then I will enter his house and dine with him and he with me." He doesn't promise everything will be wonderful in this world if we respond to his call, for: "If anyone would come after me, let him take up his cross and follow me." But for those who do respond, he promises "I will be with you always." "I will not leave you orphans." In a special way he invites us to begin enjoying the wonderful banquet heaven will provide when he tells us, "Unless you eat the flesh of the son of man and drink his blood you do not have life in you." He invites us each morning to "take this and eat, take this and drink." For Catholics this is part of his invitation to "Keep holy the Lord's day."

You might say that's a commandment, not an invitation. Yes, he does command us because we don't always feel like doing what we should, but today he invites us for he wants us to come to him not just because we're commanded, but he wants us to come because we want to, he wants us to come out of love.

There is one part of the parable that puzzle many people and that is the last part about the wedding garment. Some scholars have suggested that wedding garments were provided to guests as they arrived because the king, apparently a kind and generous man, would not have responded with such anger if they were not extremely important and easily obtainable. Jesus uses this part of the parable to warn his followers that even though a person says they believe in him, it's not going to help them much if they do not put their faith into action.

Our new age theology wants us to think that everyone is going to be blessed in the next life. Jesus is telling us eternal happiness is not to be taken for granted. The way to eternal happiness is open for all, but we have a free will as to how we will respond. May the banquet we come to today, eating his body and drinking his blood, lead us to the eternal banquet he has prepared for us. Amen.

29th Sunday Ordinary Time
October 16, 2005

INTRODUCTION – (Isaiah 45:1, 4-6; Mt. 22: 15-21) The Babylonians lived in the land we now know as Iraq, 600 years before Christ. The capital city of Babylon was just less than 100 miles south of modern day Baghdad. 587 years before Christ the Babylonians conquered the Jews and enslaved most of the Jews and took them as captives to Babylon. At that time the Persians lived in modern day Iran. Fifty years after the Babylonians conquered the Jews, the Persians conquered the Babylonians. The Persian king, Cyrus, allowed the Jews to return to their Israel. He even encouraged them to rebuild their temple to Yahweh. The prophet Isaiah, in today's first reading, sees the hand of God at work in all these events. He calls this pagan king, Cyrus, God's anointed. And although Cyrus thought it was by his own strength and shrewdness that he conquered the Babylonians, Isaiah said this was God's doings. Isaiah stresses the absolute supremacy of God, a theme in today's liturgy.

HOMILY – There were some scientists and biologists who thought they had found the secret of life. And they decided to tell God he was no longer needed. They said they could create life also. God said "well, I created life from a hand full of dirt." They said we could too. Then they picked up a hand full of dirt and started to show God what they could do. God said to them, "wait just a minute. Create your own dirt."

In today's gospel, the enemies of Jesus thought they really had Jesus in trouble this time. The gospel tells us he was approached by Pharisees and Herodians. These two groups were bitter enemies. Israel was under Roman rule, as you know, and the Herodians were totally loyal to Rome. They would have immediately accused Jesus of promoting civil rebellion and revolution if he had said "don't pay the taxes." The Pharisees, on the other hand, held that God alone was their king and Lord and they viewed the payment of taxes to Rome as caving in to the hated Roman emperor, Tiberius Caesar, a foreigner and a pagan at that! This hot issue was made worse by the fact that Rome's tax burden on the Jewish people was extremely heavy. Jesus asked them to show him a Roman coin; apparently he didn't have one. The fact that they could produce one gave evidence that, like it or not, they participated in Rome's commerce and economy. Jesus' answer to their question is well known, "Give back to Caesar the things that are Caesar's, and to God the things that are God's."

Jesus avoided getting caught in their trap. He reminded us we have obligations to both God and civil authority. We need good leadership in our country and in the countries of the world. With good leadership the citizenship will prosper. Without it the people will suffer. St. Paul even reminds us to pray for our leaders and obey them. (1 Tim 2:2 and Rom 13). In this particular confrontation, Jesus did imply that since the people chose to participate in the Roman economy, they had obligations there. But Jesus did not answer how we are to treat some of those thorny issues that we have to deal with in a society that believes in the separation of Church and State.

We have to figure out most of those issues ourselves, taking a cue from other things Jesus taught us, especially from his teaching that obeying God is our greatest responsibility. When we break the laws of our country, we get arrested or fined or have to pay some consequence. When we break God's laws, however, God doesn't come knocking on our door ready to fine us or lock us up in jail. If he did, people wouldn't get by with a lot of the things they do. But God isn't in the business of being a policeman. Rather he is interested in having us love him and doing right because of love. And love cannot be forced; it must be given freely. God could have made us all robots and we would have done exactly what he wanted us to do, but if we were robots we would not be human nor would we be capable of love. When God gave us a free will, God took a big chance that we might choose not to love him. Apparently he thought it was worth taking that chance.

Give back to God what is God's, Jesus tells us. Because God does not come knocking on our doors when we do not give him what we owe him, it's easy for us to say I'll pray later, or I'll go to church next week or I'll be good later! Later may not come for any of us. Nothing is more important than our relationship with God. Some day we will leave behind all the other things that we think are so important, and the only thing we will have left is the love for God and for others that we have demonstrated in our daily lives. That love will grow and develop only by prayer and good works.

In our society, which wants immediate results, many important things in life do not give immediate pay offs. When we plant a seed in the ground, it doesn't produce fruit the next day. If we buy stock in a good company today, it probably won't go up 50 points tomorrow. A good education takes many years before it pays dividends. The things we do to serve and obey our God are an investment, an investment that will bless us in this present life, but the full rewards of such a life are off in the future. As St. Paul tells us "eye has not seen, nor ear heard, nor has it entered into our hearts what things God has prepared for those who love him." (1 Cor 2:9) What God asks of us is simple: prayer, obedience, love, love for God and for each other. In line with prayer, we cannot neglect the most important prayer we have, the Eucharist. "Do this in memory of me," he said. That's why we're here today, to give to God our ears to listen, our hearts to be united with him, our gratitude, our expressions of faith as we praise him and receive him.

We will get in trouble with the law if we do not give back to Caesar the things that are Caesar's, but we have the most to lose if we do not give back to God the things that are God's. Our eternal happiness

30th Sunday in Ordinary Time
October 23, 2011

HOMILY – (Exodus 22:20-26; 1 Thes 1:5c-10; Matthew 22:34-40) When a woman teacher became engaged, one of her more experienced co-workers decided to give her some good advice. "Just remember, she said, the first ten years of marriage are the hardest." The younger teacher asked her co-worker how long she had been married. "Ten years," she answered. (from *Reader's Digest, Laughter, the Best Medicine*, pg. 161)

Our first reading and gospel present us with a very challenging topic: love. When we hear that word, we automatically think of romance, joy, and warm feelings. Sometimes it is; sometimes it's a matter of dedication, loyalty and commitment. Those who have matured in learning about love know that sometimes it's easy and sometimes it's hard work.

The Jewish leaders considered there were 613 precepts or commands in their law, the part of the Bible we call the "Old Testament." Jewish rabbis often debated which of these was the most important. So Jesus was asked what is the greatest. He states two, not one, as basic and central to everything else. The first is from the Book of Deuteronomy. It is part of a Scripture text that pious Jews recited twice a day. The second is from the Book of Leviticus. Putting these two together is original with Jesus and stresses Jesus' emphasis that true religion is more than a matter of external observance (which it is of course) but comes from the disposition of our hearts. Now, this topic about the interior dispositions of our hearts deserves a whole homily by itself, but it will have to wait for another time.

Right now I want to stress the importance of the external observance of God's law, that is, doing what God wants us to, even if we don't feel like it, even if our heart is not in it. I think many people in today's world think that love of God is just a matter of warm fuzzy thoughts and feelings about God, without much attention to our behavior as to whether we are doing what God wants us to do. For example, taking seriously the Commandment of keeping holy the Lord's day, taking any time for worship or serious prayer, many consider unnecessary. Jesus said in John's gospel: "if you love me you will keep my commandments." (Jn. 14:15)

Notice which of these two commandments of love of

God and neighbor Jesus said is the first and the greatest. But the second is like it and we can't really love God whom we do not see if we do not love our neighbor whom we do see (1 John 4:20). There are almost an infinite number of ways we can love others: from common ordinary decency and friendliness to really putting ourselves out for those who are the most destitute as St. Francis or Mother Teresa did. This week, however, I would like to make a special reference to a man who had a great love for the people of Cincinnati: Carl Lindner. I have to mention him because he was such a special help to me while I was taking care of St. Joseph Church a few years ago. When I was assigned to pastor St. Joseph's Church temporarily (for three years), I discovered that Mr. Lindner had made a generous donation the previous year to St. Joe's at Christmas time. I got the idea that maybe with a special request, he would do more. How does a person get to see such an important figure as Carl Lindner? I didn't know how to reach him, but a good friend told me to go downtown to his office and ask to see him. So I stirred up the courage to do that. I went to his office building and asked the receptionist if I could talk with him. I was sent to a waiting room, offered something to drink, and waited about 15-20 minutes and Carl Lindner came walking in with a couple of his staff members. He met with me for a little while, showed much interest in what I was doing and asked questions about St. Joe's Church and about its school. He offered to help me out and, subsequently, sent a donation 10 times what he had given in the past – which was considerable. Of course, I went back to thank him after we received it and every year after that he helped St. Joe and kept us out of the red. I felt this should be mentioned, because I'm sure he did lots of charity like that, things no one ever heard about. It was indeed a privilege to have known him. He was a Baptist, as most of you probably know, but he told me his mother was Catholic. I think that was why he was generous to Catholic organizations. One time when I went to thank him for his help, he said to me, "you know I help many people around the city and so few bother to say 'thanks.'" I was surprised to hear that, but I shouldn't have been surprised. It corresponds with the gospel story about Jesus healing the ten lepers, and only one returning to say "thanks."

That is why we are here today – to say "thanks" to God for all his goodness to us. The word "Eucharist" means "thanksgiving." We thank God for people like Carl Lindner as well as for people who have far fewer resources than he did but whose hearts are also generous and giving. I know many like that here at St. Boniface. Giving God thanks is an important part of our love for God. St. Paul tells us as much in Colossians: "Whatever you do, in word or deed, do everything in the name of the Lord Jesus, giving thanks to God the Father through him." (Colossians 3:17)

31st Sunday in Ordinary Time
October 30, 2011

INTRODUCTION – (Malachi 1:14b-2:2b, 8-10; Matthew 23:1-12) Our first reading is from the Book of the Prophet Malachi. In most bibles this is the last book in the Old Testament. Malachi was a fire and brimstone prophet who lived about 450 or 500 years before Christ. We don't know his real name because the word "Malachi" means "my messenger." In today's passage the prophet is mostly condemning the sins of the priests. The last verse of our reading is addressed to the people. What are those sins? Further on in his message, Malachi gives detailed descriptions of their sins, such as offering sacrifices unworthy of God. When a person brought an animal to the Temple, such as a lamb or an ox, to have the priest offer it in sacrifice, often the animal was blind, lame and sick. It was the law that only a perfect offering be offered, so the priest probably had to be given a bribe to offer such an imperfect sacrifice. Malachi said offer that sick or blind animal as a gift to your governor and see if he would be pleased. Other than condemning their unworthy worship of God, Malachi condemned the priests for not teaching the people what was right. One such thing the priests were telling the people was "Every evildoer is good in the sight of the Lord, and God is pleased with him." (Mal. 2:17) It sounds very much like new age theology doesn't it? In the last verse of today's reading, Malachi turns his focus to the people and chastises them for breaking God's covenant through sins of adultery, dishonesty and injustice. The reading prepares us for the gospel where Jesus, God's prophet, condemns the Jewish leaders of his day.

HOMILY – An employee at a local company suffered from an immense superiority complex. She usually had low-level jobs and one day found herself moved up to a little higher position with a cubicle of her own. That really inflated her ego. While she was still getting settled, she saw a man approaching her work area. Immediately she picked up the phone and pretended to be on an important phone call. "Yes, J.D." she said, loud enough to be heard by anyone 50 feet away, (J.D. were the initials of the president of the company) "thank you for your kind wishes and I will take care of what you asked me to do right away." Then she hung up the phone, turned in her swivel chair with an air of importance and said to the man standing at her door: "May I help you?" "I'm sorry to disturb you," he said. "I'm here to hook up your phone." Jesus tells us, "whoever exalts himself will be humbled, and whoever humbles himself will be exalted." (adapted from *Preaching Resources* 31st Sunday in Ordinary Time.)

We just heard strong condemnations from the prophet called Malachi of the priests of his day and Jesus' condemnation of the scribes and Pharisees of his time. The condemnations were well justified for these groups of religious leaders thought they were so great, while they were full of pride and lacking in true holiness. In the history of all religions, it has always caused great damage to people's faith and to the Church when its leaders failed to live virtuous lives. Yet we are all human and, along with the entire gathering of Christ's followers, we confess that we are sinners as we ask God's mercy each time we begin the Mass.

But today's Scripture readings apply not only to religious leaders. Every person has a circle of people around them whom they influence for better or for worse. Certainly with people at work, in our neighborhoods, in our families, we can be a good influence or a bad influence. We used to call it setting a good example or being a bad example. Even though we do not hear these terms very often any more, they are still realities. Even children in a family or in school can be a good influence or bad influence on each other.

The kinds of things we say, the encouragement we give to do right or wrong, can make us true leaders for good or for no good. But do we go around like an Old Testament prophet pointing out people's faults when we see them doing wrong? It's a delicate thing. Some people can do it effectively, some people just alienate the people they are trying to help. Recently, I heard a good answer to the question St. Francis gave a person when the person told Francis that he often sees people doing wrong. He asked Francis, "should I tap people on the shoulder and tell them that they should be acting differently?" Francis said, "Do you live a good life, love your family, worship God, help others, then you are preaching to others how a person should live."

My most sincere prayer every day is "Lord, help me be useful to you." Some day, when I stand before the Lord, I know he will not find me perfect, but I hope he will say to me: "you were a big help to me in bringing the message of my love to others." Amen.

All Saints
November 1, 2005

INTRODUCTION – Our first reading is from the book of Revelation (Rev. 7:2-4, 9-14). The section just preceding today's passage described the end of the world. The sun became dark and the moon became red as blood and there was a great earthquake all over the earth. People tried to hide from all these terrible things and they asked: "Who can survive?" Today's reading answers the question: those who have followed Christ faithfully. And those who have followed Christ faithfully form a large crowd which no one could count. The number 144,000 is a symbolic number, symbolic of completion or perfection.

HOMILY – (Gospel: Matthew 5:1-12a) Do you ever notice all the saints we have represented here at St. Boniface church? There is the Blessed Virgin altar and St. Joseph's altar with their statues. There are statues of St. Anthony, St. Rita, St. Teresa (aka, the Little Flower), St. Patrick and St. John Vianney (in the back). Someone asked where is the statue of St. Boniface. It's outside at the top of the front of the church. There are those in the stained glass windows: Sts. Martha and

Mary, all the apostles, St. Boniface, St. Cecilia and St. Gregory the Great in the stained glass windows in the choir loft. There are thousands of others who are designated as "saints" in the Church. I have a book that lists 7000 "saints" and says a little bit about each one of them. Today's first reading tells us about a crowd so large that no one could count them. Who could count how many people there were who have lived holy lives and gone to heaven throughout these past 2000 years? I would have a hard time counting all the wonderful people I have known as a priest whom I'm sure God has welcomed into his kingdom.

We can learn a lot from all these holy people. Among them were people who died young and those who died old, those who were married, those who were single and those who were religious or priests. There were people from every walk of life, wealthy people and poor people and people in-between. Even though they had so many differences among them, they had certain things in common. They believed in God's love, they made loving God central in their own lives. Some even went so far as to suffer martyrdom rather than give up their commitment to God. They revered the Mass, the sacraments and the Scriptures. They loved others not just in an emotional sort of way but in a way so as to be of service and help to others. In today's feast, the Church not only wants us to remember all these holy people, but the Church puts them before us as guides on our own way to God. And it gives us the comfort of knowing that our relatives and friends who have gone before us and who have died in God's grace now enjoy the fullness of God's life and God's joy. Some of the saints, as we know, were not holy at all in their younger days, but they came to realize the error of their ways and turned their lives around, knowing God is always ready for us to turn back to him if we will.

God has called us all to a life of holiness. God has called us all to be saints. If we end up being pictured in some stained glass window in a church that might be nice, but what is really important is that we be among that great number in God's heavenly kingdom. St. John tells us in today's second reading (1 Jn 3:1–3) that in God's love he has made us his children. We are not only called God's children but that's what we really are. We ask the Lord today to help us realize our dignity and our purpose to be God's children for all eternity with God in heaven.

All Souls
November 2, 2008

INTRODUCTION – (2 Maccabees 12:43-46; Romans 5:5-11; John 6:37-40) Our first reading, from the book of Maccabees, comes from about 100 years before Christ. At that time in history the Greeks were the dominant power and they were trying to get the Jews to abandon their faith and follow the beliefs of the pagans. Those who would not give in were persecuted and put to death. The loyal Jews fought back. In one of their battles, many Jews were killed. As they were being buried, it was found that they had small statues of pagan gods attached to their garments. These Jews were loyal to their Jewish beliefs, but they had, to some extent, given in to paganism. Just in case those pagan gods were real, they were carrying with them statues of pagan gods to give them protection. Their leader, Judas Maccabeus, took up a collection to send to Jerusalem for sacrifices to be offered up to the Lord for those people. He believed their hearts were, in general, in the right place, but for the weakness in their faith they had to be forgiven. In this piece of history from 100 B.C., we can see the beginnings of the belief that our prayers can help those who have died, a belief that is still part of our faith.

HOMILY – Praying for our deceased relatives and friends is what our feast of All Souls is about today. However, I had the hardest time getting started with today's homily. I kept putting it off. It's not as if I do not believe in praying for friends and relatives who have died. I do it all the time and it has been a tradition in the Church from the beginning, and even before that as we heard in our first reading.

I think the difficulty I had in developing my homily comes from two sources. First, many people don't like to hear about death and what might come afterwards. We know we can't avoid it, but my sense is that many people believe that if they don't think about it, it won't happen, at least not for a long time. My suspicion is that my father was that way. I constantly tried to get him to make a will but he never did. As a CPA he would have known it was a good idea. I think making a will would have made the prospect of his own death too concrete and too real for him to deal with.

The second reason today's homily was hard was that I would have to talk about Purgatory. It's an idea that many Christians deny. I remember once I was helping a family prepare the liturgy for their deceased father and they insisted "absolutely no mention of Purgatory." It's as if it were a bad word. They wanted to think their father was perfect, I guess, and was already in heaven. Most of us would like to believe that our loved ones go straight to heaven when they die – period. If this were true, then they would not need our prayers. If they went to the other place, God forbid, our prayers would do them no good. The Church teaches, in every Mass we have for a person who died and in today's feast, that our prayers do help our relatives and friends who have left this world as they journey to eternal life.

Purgatory, among all the mysteries and beliefs of the Church is an extremely logical and comforting doctrine. It's logical if we ask ourselves how many of us think we will be perfect when we die. There may even be some who are perfect right now. I would ask them to identify themselves, but if they're perfect, they will also be too humble to do so. Even those who lived a good life may still have a little room for improvement, they may still not love God or others quite enough. That's where Purgatory comes in – it's an opportunity to grow into the most loving, most holy person we can possibly be. As a result we would then be filled with God's peace and joy and love to the fullest extent. Luther rejected the idea of Purgatory because of the abuse of indulgences at the time. Today, the concept of Purgatory has been rejected by many because of all the negative images of suffering and punishment that we grew up with. Actually, I think for the souls in Purgatory, happiness far outweighs the unhappiness. Their salvation is sure, they are more closely united with God than they had ever experienced before in their lives, they are on their way to the enjoyment of God's kingdom in the fullest possible way. But they're not there yet and that's the painful part.

If you read the book, "The Five People You Meet in Heaven," I think you get a good, practical image of Purgatory. It's not a religious book, it's very entertaining and it pictured for me what Purgatory might be like as we work out issues, regrets, hurts, conflicts, etc., that we might take with us when we die.

To demonstrate that Purgatory makes so much sense, I think that those who deny Purgatory have had to find a substitute for it in their thinking about the next life. For many that substitute is reincarnation. In reincarnation a person supposedly keeps working for greater and greater purity and holiness until they are ready to be perfectly one with God. However, reincarnation comes from Hinduism. Actually a Hindu does not look forward to reincarnation because they don't want to have to pass through this world of pain and suffering one more time. I suspect the notion of reincarnation has been adopted by many Westerners, even Christians, because it fits our culture of "buy now, pay later." They figure they can live any way they want and can postpone having to pay any consequences. Our faith tells us, "now is the acceptable time, now is the day of salvation." God gives us what we need in this life to help us know him and serve him in this life. If we do not do it perfectly, Purgatory is there to finish the job. Today, we renew our faith in life after death. Today too we renew our belief in the power of prayer to help our loved ones, even those who are no longer among us, for in Christ they are still one with us. With Christ our great high priest, we offer now the greatest prayer there is, the Eucharist.

32nd Sunday in Ordinary Time
November 6, 2011

INTRODUCTION – (Wisdom 6:12-16; Matthew 25: 1-13) Greece has fallen on bad times lately, but centuries ago, it was the center of culture and civilization. Alexander the Great, who was born in 357 BC, had conquered the entire Middle East by the time of his death at age 34: from Greece and Egypt all the way to India. (It took him 13 years) Under his generals, the Greek language and Greek culture supplanted the local culture. This is the situation at the time the Book of Wisdom was written. Wisdom literature in the Middle East is very ancient, going back almost 1000 years before Christ. The wisdom literature of the various nations expressed practical insights about manners, morality and the mysteries of life. Jewish wisdom writings took many of these insights and combined them with the wisdom in God's law. With wisdom from the Scriptures, Jewish wisdom offered a more profound view of life and how to live it. Our first reading from the Book of Wisdom was written perhaps about 50 years before Christ, probably in Alexandria in Egypt. It was written in the language of those times, Greek. Since it was not composed in Hebrew, you will not find it in the Protestant Bible. The Catholic Church, however, accepts it as inspired. Our first reading tells us wisdom is available for anyone who diligently seeks it with honesty and openness. But those who find the search for wisdom too much trouble will be deprived of it. A theme we hear again in the gospel.

HOMILY – I hate to tell an old joke but this one fits today's gospel. Fr. Murphy paid a visit to one of his elderly parishioners whom he hadn't seen at church for a few months. In a nice way, he tried to tell her she should be coming to church. "You know," he said, "you are not getting any younger and you should start thinking more of the hereafter." "Well, Father," she said, "I think of the hereafter all the time." I go into the kitchen and I say to myself, what am I here after. And I go into the bedroom and I ask myself, what am I here after. And it's goes on like that all day."

In the next few weeks Jesus will be trying to get us to think more about the hereafter. The year is coming to an end (a new Church year begins in three weeks) and our life in this world will come to an end too. We're not going to dwell in this world forever. God has other plans for us and he wants us to be in on them. Several times this year, I have mentioned that Jesus' message is an apocalyptic message. He has come to reveal to us the Kingdom of God and he wants us to be part of that

Kingdom. It is a kingdom where God will be in charge, a kingdom which Jesus has used many images to describe. Today the kingdom is compared to a wedding party. Weddings in the Middle East might be celebrated for several days. The celebration began with dancing and entertainment as the guests awaited the arrival of the groom. Punctuality was not an important element of their culture. Perhaps the groom was having his own party with his friends. Usually, however, the groom was busy haggling with the parents of the bride over the gifts he was expected to give to the relatives of the bride. Late night weddings were common. As Jesus tells the story, the bride is not mentioned, nor are we told where the guests had gathered, nor where everyone would process to in the middle of the night with their torches for the wedding and for more celebration. All these unanswered questions are not relevant to the main point of the story. The story is not about the details of the wedding, it is about the Kingdom of God and the virgins represent the Church. The wise virgins anticipated a delay and were prepared. It should be added also that the parable is not about sharing, the oil represents something unable to be shared, something entirely personal. The parable is about being prepared for the sudden arrival of the groom (in the lesson of Jesus, the unknown time when the groom will arrive represents the suddenness when Christ will come and call us into his kingdom). The closed door represents that if we are not prepared, it will be too late for us. We will miss the celebration of eternal life God has invited us to.

In my meditation on this gospel, it struck me what a terrible feeling it is to be unprepared. Whenever I'm under a lot of stress, I always dream of being in a situation where I'm unprepared. I dream I'm back in school and there is a test coming up and I didn't study for it. Or I dream I'm getting up to read the gospel or to preach and I can't find the gospel in the book or I can't find my homily notes. I keep looking around as people start leaving. And pretty soon, there's no one left in church and I'm still looking. In our busy lives, we have to constantly remember what is most important, and being prepared to meet our God is the most important. That is the whole purpose of our having been created, to be with God forever.

Whether it is the devil or our own tendency to procrastinate, but something keeps telling us we have plenty of time to prepare. We think we have too many other things to worry about right now. This is definitely a lack of wisdom with regard to something as important as our eternal salvation. Or another thing we keep hearing, especially in today's culture, is that everyone is getting into heaven anyway, no matter how we've lived or what we've done. That's not the message Jesus gives us. He tells us over and over again in many ways: "You know neither the day nor the hour," so the moral is be wise and be prepared. Amen.

Dedication of St. John Lateran
November 9, 2008

INTRODUCTION – (Ezekiel 47:1-2,8-9,12, 1 Corinthians 3:9c-11,16-17, John 2:13-22) The celebration of the dedication of the Church of St. John Lateran in Rome is a universal feast of the Church. It is the oldest Catholic Church in Rome and it is the Cathedral Church of the Holy Father. Actually the popes lived there for 1000 years and it is still considered the Pope's cathedral. In a sense it symbolizes all existing churches in the world today.

Our first reading is a vision of the prophet Ezekiel who had lots of visions and recorded them. At the time this vision took place, Jerusalem and its Temple had been destroyed by the Babylonians. The prophet sees that one day the city would be restored and the temple would be rebuilt. It is an idealized temple he sees. There is a stream of water flowing from the temple, flowing east and south toward the desert of the Arabah and into the Dead Sea. The water in the Dead Sea is seven times more salty than the ocean and nothing can live in it. In Ezekiel's vision, however, the water that flows from the temple gives life to everything it comes in contact with and even makes the Dead Sea into fresh water. The meaning is that what flows from God's house, prayer and sacrifice and worship is life giving. The book of Revelations takes up this image, for the vision is still waiting to be fulfilled.

HOMILY – Buildings are important not just to keep us warm and dry. They are important for many, many reasons. Winston Churchill said it so clearly when London had to be rebuilt after the World War II. "We shape our buildings then our buildings shape our lives." Today we celebrate the dedication of a church building. A church building is a holy place, a place where God's people gather for prayer and worship and sacrifice. Jesus' reaction to the abuses in the Temple shows us God's house should be treated as a holy place.

But a church building is important not just because God is there but because we are. A church building is called a church only because it is where the Church gathers and prays and celebrates God's saving love. Without the gathering of God's people, it would not be a church, even if it were the most beautiful building ever built. Today's celebration reminds us the Church is first and foremost the community of God's people, for the

Church existed for almost 300 years before the first building was built. Before then the Church met in people's homes or during times of persecution they met in catacombs in order to pray and celebrate the Eucharist. Notice that gathering together was so important that the early Christians would risk their lives in order to do so. When Constantine became emperor he issued the edict of toleration thus ending the persecution. It was he who built St. John Lateran. So today's commemoration of St. John Lateran is a feast worth celebrating; it's also a feast reminding us that Church is more than a place to go. It is all of us who gather together here or anywhere else God's people come together to pray.

So many people today claim to belong to a Church, but they are seldom there. I think they deceive themselves to say they belong to a Church unless they belong to the gathering of God's people. That's what Church really is. In the second reading St. Paul says, "You are God's building." Those who are physically unable to be part of the gathering because of sickness or infirmity are still connected with us through the Eucharist our Communion ministers take to them each week. Belonging to a Church is more than having your name on a church's roster or in the church's computer. Being part of a church involves more than simply believing in Christ. St. James tells us the devils also believe…and tremble with fear. (James 2:19) Later on in his letter, Paul uses another example to show that following Christ means being part of a community of believers. He tells us we are all members of Christ's body and we need to be united and work together as one. Certainly, coming together in prayer and worship is an expression of our oneness in Christ. (It would be nice if we showed this oneness by coming closer to the altar when we come to pray and not spread all over church. But that's another issue.)

Sometimes it's hard to be part of a community each week. We can all find reasons why we're too busy to get to church. We live in a society that promotes the attitude that we can make up our own rules. When we're part of a community, not everyone is as perfect as we are. There are scandals and there is hypocrisy in the Church. I always remind people of the statement by Fr. Greeley: "If you ever find a perfect church, by all means join it. Just know that once you join it, it will no longer be perfect." The Church has been scarred with failures and sins from the time Judas betrayed Christ and Peter denied him. But Christ hasn't given up on his Church and continues to be with us and to call us to holiness. He promised he will be with us always until the end of time. We continue to offer our prayers asking God to bless us as his people gathered in faith. Amen.

33rd Sunday in Ordinary Time
November 13, 2011

HOMILY – (Proverbs 31:10-13, 19-20, 30-31; 1 Thes 5:1-6; Mt 25:14-30) In two weeks we are celebrating the beginning of a new Church year with the first Sunday of Advent. We begin again to tell the story of Jesus, his birth, his ministry of teaching, healing, forgiving and exorcisms, his saving death, resurrection, ascension and his sending the Holy Spirit upon us. We will also begin to use a new translation for the prayers in the Roman Missal at Mass. This is what I want to talk about today.

When I said my first Mass in May, 1964, it was a traditional Latin Mass. Even the Scripture readings were first read in Latin and then they were repeated in English before the sermon. In Advent that same year, we began to say some of the parts of the Mass in English. For me that was refreshing and exciting. I had studied Latin for seven and a half years and I sat through two years of a course in St. Thomas Aquinas' Summa when the teacher taught in Latin and the tests were essay tests in Latin. Even with that background, I found myself more often translating the prayers of the Mass and of the Divine Office rather than really praying them. Gradually more and more of the Mass was prayed in our own language. The first official translation of the entire Mass into English came out in 1974. A second edition came out in 1985. It is that translation we have been using for the past 25 or 26 years. Pope John Paul and the International Congregation for English in the Liturgy felt that this 1985 translation was missing some of the dignity, beauty, doctrinal precision, nuances and poetic expressions of the Latin prayers, so a new translation was ordered. Our style of prayer for the past two dozen years expressed a certain familiarity with God; however, not to the extent of walking up to greet God and saying, "Hi, God, how are ya'?" Yet our prayer is almost conversational and comfortable. The Church wants our prayers to reflect to a greater degree how awesome God is. For example, we will usually say "O God" rather than simply "God" when we address God; or another example we will frequently hear in our prayers "we humbly beseech you" rather than simply telling God what we expect God to do for us. The new text also tries to render accurately words and phrases that we find in the Scriptures. I think these are all good things. One other good thing about the new translation is, because it is new, we will hear and pray the prayers with greater attention, at least for a while.

One of the speakers we had on the new translation

gave us the example of Lincoln's Gettysburg address, which many of us memorized in grade school: "Four score and seven years ago ..." It is a speech that is literary and even poetic. The same things could have been said in a more mundane way. Lincoln could have said: "Eighty seven years ago our ancestors started this country because they wanted to be free and because they believed we're all equal. Now our Country has been in a big fight over these principals, etc. etc." The point I am trying to make is the same thing can be said in different ways. Our new translation purports to be a more beautiful, dignified, humble, nuanced expression of the original Latin prayers.

We will have a prayer card in the pews in two weeks. You will be able to easily follow the prayers and all the changes are printed in bold print. I'm not going to comment on all the changes right now. After we get familiar with the new wording, I will offer a more detailed explanation. Right now I just want to point out a couple of things that will immediately strike you. This will probably be the hardest thing to get used to at first: when the priest says "The Lord be with you." You answer "And with your spirit." For those of you who remember when the Mass was in Latin, this was the response: "Et cum spiritu tuo." This response reflects the language St. Paul uses at the end of four of his letters. Before the gospel, when the priest or deacon announces, "A reading from the holy gospel according to Mark," you answer, "Glory to you O Lord." (That is the O inserted before Lord that I mentioned earlier).

There are other changes you will notice. If you want to read more about it, there is an insert in today's bulletin with a good explanation of most of the changes in detail. If you still want to read more, there are a few booklets on the radiators. They do a very good job explaining the new translation.

Some people love change; some people hate it. It will be that way with this until we all grow comfortable with it. A year from now, it will all come automatically. I like it that the wording is more scriptural; that the attitude behind the prayers expresses the greatness of God and how privileged we are to enter into God's presence. Stay tuned for more information in a month or two. Amen.

Christ the King
November 20, 2011

INTRODUCTION – (Ezekiel 34:11-12, 15-17; 1 Cor. 15:20-26, 28; Matthew 25:31-46) Today we honor Christ as our King. Our scripture readings do not picture him as a typical king. In our first reading, Ezekiel, the prophet, pictures God as a shepherd. God is distressed with the shepherds of his people; i.e., the kings and religious leaders. They led God's people away from God and to eventual disaster when the Babylonians invaded. God said he himself would lead them rightly. We see this prophecy perfectly fulfilled in Jesus. In our second reading, the whole chapter from Paul's First Letter to the Corinthians, from which our reading is taken is on the topic of the resurrection. Paul tells us the risen Jesus will reign until evil in every form has been destroyed. Then Jesus will turn the kingdom over to the Father. In the gospel Jesus is pictured as a judge, a judge who judges us on how we behave toward the lowly and the poor. Thus we have three images of Christ the King: a shepherd, the risen Lord and the judge of all nations.

HOMILY – Before Mass we projected on our screen the central part of Michelangelo's famous painting of the Last Judgment in the Sistine Chapel. The painting was based on today's gospel of Jesus judging the nations. This is one of the most powerful and one of the most memorable of Jesus' parables. The image of Jesus saying, "Depart from me you accursed?" is a picture of Jesus we would prefer not to think of (unless he is saying it to someone we greatly dislike). When we think of Jesus in relation to ourselves, we would rather picture him as kind, loving and forgiving. As judge he administers both forgiveness and justice. Today's parable repeats a theme that is found in many other parables, parables that tell us this is a time to come to him for forgiveness and mercy. Then there will come a time when it will be too late: a time when God will ask us to give an accounting of ourselves. We see this theme in the parable of the talents, the parable of the five wise and five foolish virgins, the parable of the workers in the vineyard, the parable of the great wedding feast where those invited offered lame excuses for why they could not come, as well as the part about the guest without the wedding garment, the parable of the unforgiving steward, the parable of the unjust steward and the parable about the rich man and Lazarus, just to mention a few that immediately come to mind.

If it disturbs us to think of Jesus as a judge who can condemn as well as forgive, than we can remember what Jesus said in John's gospel: "I came not to condemn the world but to save the world." (Jn. 12:47). He goes on to say, "the one who rejects me and does not receive my word has something to judge him; on the last day the word that I have spoken will serve as judge." (Jn. 12:48). In other words, the way we live will catch up with us. There is karma in the universe. The good we have done, the good we haven't done and the evil we have done will judge us; Jesus will not have to. There is no getting around that. Now is the time for forgiveness. Now is the time to start over, (in the language of the gospel, the time for conversion). We've seen many TV shows of judges sitting in a courtroom handing out reward or punishment. I believe that in the final analysis, when the time comes for us to stand before Jesus, he will not be like a judge sitting in a courtroom. It will be the love that is in us, the love for God and the love for others that will determine whether our eternity will be an eternity of peace and joy or an eternity full of regret for having thrown away the opportunities God gave us to know him and love him and love others.

The truth Jesus teaches in today's parable is reflected in the real life experience of the conversion of St. Paul. When Paul, before his conversion, was persecuting the Christians and was on his way to Damascus to arrest Christians and bring them back to Jerusalem for trial, Jesus appeared to him in a blinding light. Paul asked, "Who are you, Lord?" Jesus answered, "I am Jesus, whom you are persecuting." What Paul was doing to Jesus' followers, he was doing to Jesus. A powerful image! It is this concept that inspired many saints to dedicate themselves to minister to the poor and suffering such as Mother Theresa, St. Martin de Porres, Damian the leper, St. Vincent de Paul, St. Francis Xavier Cabrini, St. Katherine Drexel, St. Peter Claver, and many others

What you do to the least of my brothers and sisters you do to me. This does not imply that we can ignore our obligation to worship, praise and thank God. It is, after all, the first and greatest commandment to love God above all things. Today we are reminded how important the second commandment is, which is like the first: to love our neighbor as ourselves. Loving God, loving Jesus inspires us to love our neighbor for when we love another, relative, friend, associate, even someone who dislikes us or whom we dislike, especially if they are truly needy, we are loving Jesus. Amen.

"This is My Body, This is My Blood."

Prayer Before the
Holy Sacrifice of the Mass

Let me be a holy sacrifice and unite with God in the sacrament of His greatest love.

I want to be one in Him in this act of love, where He gives Himself to me and I give myself as a sacrifice to Him. Let me be a holy sacrifice as I become one with Him in this my act of greatest love to Him.

Let me unite with Him more, that I may more deeply love Him. May I help make reparation to His adorable Heart and the heart of His Mother, Mary. With greatest love, I offer myself to You and pray that You will accept my sacrifice of greatest love. I give myself to You and unite in Your gift of Yourself to me. Come and possess my soul.

Cleanse me, strengthen me, heal me. Dear Holy Spirit act in the heart of Mary to make me more and more like Jesus.

Father, I offer this my sacrifice, myself united to Jesus in the Holy Spirit to You. Help me to love God more deeply in this act of my greatest love.

Give me the grace to grow in my knowledge, love and service of You and for this to be my greatest participation in the Mass. Give me the greatest graces to love You so deeply in this Mass, You who are so worthy of my love.

– *Mass Book*, December 27, 1995

My dear beloved priests,

I give my heart to Jesus and Mary with you in love.

Stay with Me one hour and feel my power.

We want Adoration Chapels around the world.

From Fr. Edward Carter, S.J., 1996 –
The Eucharist is the Bread of Life –

Apostles of the Eucharistic Heart of Jesus

There is a new prayer movement which has been started under the direction of Shepherds of Christ Ministries. We are asking for volunteers who are willing to pray before the Blessed Sacrament for one hour, twice-weekly. Members of the Shepherds of Christ prayer chapters, as well as others, are to be invited to join this movement.

These apostles are to pray for the intentions given.

For part of the hour they are to use the prayers of the Shepherds of Christ Associates Handbook. They may spend the rest of the hour as they so choose.

This new prayer movement within the Shepherds of Christ Ministries is a powerful way to help in the renewal of the Church and the world. The name, Apostles of the Eucharistic Heart of Jesus, has been given to this movement.

Rita Ring is the coordinator for this activity.

This is indeed a special calling for us to unite in one heart with His Eucharistic Heart and pray for the following intentions:

1. For the spread of the devotion to the Hearts of Jesus and Mary culminating in the reign of the Sacred Heart and the triumph of the Immaculate Heart.
2. For the Pope.
3. For all bishops of the world.
4. For all priests.
5. For all sisters and brothers in the religious life.
6. For all members of the Shepherds of Christ Movement, and for the spread of this movement to the world.
7. For all members of the Catholic Church.
8. For all members of the human family.
9. For all souls in purgatory.

We have prayer chapters praying
　　for the priests, the Church and
　　the world in 9 languages –
　　all over the world –
　　Giving great devotion to the
　　Sacred Heart and Immaculate Heart –

Please pray these prayers for the
    priests, the Church and the world –

Be an Apostle of the Eucharistic
    Heart of Jesus –
    Pray these prayers and the rosary
    before the Blessed Sacrament
    2 hours a week for the
    following intentions:

1. For the spread of the devotion to the Hearts
   of Jesus and Mary culminating in the reign
   of the Sacred Heart and the triumph of the
   Immaculate Heart.
2. For the Pope.
3. For all bishops of the world.
4. For all priests.
5. For all sisters and brothers in the religious
   life.
6. For all members of the Shepherds of Christ
   Movement, and for the spread of this
   movement to the world.
7. For all members of the Catholic Church.
8. For all members of the human family.
9. For all souls in purgatory.

Only God's grace can help us.

We must give our lives doing
    the Father's will – loving
    God and our neighbor
    united to the Masses
    going on around the world.

SAY DAILY

*GOD, I GIVE YOU MY LIFE IN UNION
WITH THE MASS AS AN OFFERING FOR
THE SOULS, THE CHURCH AND THE
PRIESTS.*

HELP US!

I see Fr. Carter, SJ. when he did his doctorate on the Sacred Heart outlined much of what he said Jesus told him to do in the Shepherds of Christ in circulating over 17,000,000 Priestly Newsletters, loose and in books, to priests and hierarchy in these 19 years we have existed.

We give you Fr. Joseph Robinson's homilies. Fr. Joe is my brother. This is his 7th book now. Last year we circulated his book to the Pope and all the Cardinals in the world and all the priests and Bishops of the United States. (over 32,000 received Fr. Joe's book last year, Cycle C – *Centered in Christ*) His book is centered on the bread of life – on the Word and the Eucharist.

John 11:25
I am the resurrection and the life.

Response in Christ

Included in this book are the Shepherds of Christ Prayers, also in the trifold brochure, (available in different languages) for the priests, the Church and the world in 9 languages with the Church's *Imprimatur*.

Mary said at Fatima until a sufficient number of people have consecrated their hearts to Jesus and Mary we won't have peace in the world. Mary said at Fatima: Bishops need to consecrate their dioceses to the Sacred Heart and Immaculate Heart – putting pictures of Jesus, the Sacred Heart and the Immaculate Heart of Mary, in their homes, businesses, Churches where Jesus is the King and Center of their hearts.

Rita Ring, Co-founder
Shepherds of Christ Ministries

Shepherds of Christ Associates

P R A Y E R   M A N U A L

Shepherds of Christ Publications
China, Indiana

Imprimi Potest: Rev. Bradley M. Schaeffer, S.J.
Provincial
Chicago Province, The Society of Jesus
Imprimatur: Most Rev. Carl K. Moeddel
Auxiliary Bishop
Archdiocese of Cincinnati

The Shepherds of Christ Associates Prayer Manual is published by
Shepherds of Christ Publications, an arm of Shepherds of Christ Ministries,
P.O. Box 627 China, Indiana 47250 USA.

Founder, Shepherds of Christ Ministries:
Father Edward J. Carter, S.J.

For more information contact:
Shepherds of Christ Associates
P.O. Box 627
China, Indiana 47250- USA
Tel. 812-273-8405
Toll Free: 1-888-211-3041
Fax 812-273-3182

First Printing, September 1994
Second Printing, November 1994
Third Printing, November 1995
Fourth Printing, March 1996

Chapter Meeting
Prayer Format

The prayer format below should be followed at chapter meetings of *Shepherds of Christ Associates*. All prayers, not just those said specifically for priests, should include the intention of praying for all the needs of priests the world over.

1. **Hymns.** Hymns may be sung at any point of the prayer part of the meeting.

2. **Holy Spirit Prayer.** Come, Holy Spirit, almighty Sanctifier, God of love, who filled the Virgin Mary with grace, who wonderfully changed the hearts of the apostles, who endowed all Your martyrs with miraculous courage, come and sanctify us. Enlighten our minds, strengthen our wills, purify our consciences, rectify our judgment, set our hearts on fire, and preserve us from the misfortunes of resisting Your inspirations. Amen.

3. **The Rosary.**

4. **Salve Regina.** "Hail Holy Queen, Mother of mercy, our life, our sweetness, and our hope. To you do we cry, poor banished children of Eve. To you do we send up our sighs, our mourning, our weeping in this vale of tears. Turn, then, most gracious advocate, your eyes of mercy toward us and after this, our exile, show unto us the blessed fruit of your womb, Jesus, O clement, O loving, O sweet Virgin Mary. Amen."

5. **The Memorare.** "Remember, O most gracious Virgin Mary, that never was it known that anyone who fled to your protection, implored your help, or sought your intercession was left unaided. Inspired by this confidence, I fly unto you, O Virgin of virgins, my

Mother. To you I come, before you I stand, sinful and sorrowful. O Mother of the Word Incarnate, despise not my petitions, but, in your mercy, hear and answer me. Amen."

6. **Seven Hail Marys in honor of the Seven Sorrows of Mary.** Mary has promised very special graces to those who do this on a daily basis. Included in the promises of Our Lady for those who practice this devotion is her pledge to give special assistance at the hour of death, including the sight of her face. The seven sorrows are:

(1) The first sorrow: the prophecy of Simeon (Hail Mary).
(2) The second sorrow: the flight into Egypt (Hail Mary).
(3) The third sorrow: the loss of the Child Jesus in the temple (Hail Mary).
(4) The fourth sorrow: Jesus and Mary meet on the way to the cross (Hail Mary).
(5) The fifth sorrow: Jesus dies on the cross (Hail Mary).
(6) The sixth sorrow: Jesus is taken down from the cross and laid in Mary's arms (Hail Mary).
(7) The seventh sorrow: the burial of Jesus (Hail Mary).

7. **Litany of the Blessed Virgin Mary.**
   Lord, have mercy on us.
   Christ, have mercy on us.
   Lord, have mercy on us. Christ, hear us.
   Christ, graciously hear us.
   God, the Father of heaven, *have mercy on us.*
   God, the Son, Redeemer of the world, *have mercy on us.*
   God, the Holy Spirit, *have mercy on us.*

Holy Trinity, one God, *have mercy on us.*
Holy Mary, *pray for us* (repeat after each invocation).
Holy Mother of God,
Holy Virgin of virgins,
Mother of Christ,
Mother of the Church,
Mother of divine grace,
Mother most pure,
Mother most chaste,
Mother inviolate,
Mother undefiled,
Mother most amiable,
Mother most admirable,
Mother of good counsel,
Mother of our Creator,
Mother of our Savior,
Virgin most prudent,
Virgin most venerable,
Virgin most renowned,
Virgin most powerful,
Virgin most merciful,
Virgin most faithful,
Mirror of justice,
Seat of wisdom,
Cause of our joy,
Spiritual vessel,
Vessel of honor,
Singular vessel of devotion,
Mystical rose,
Tower of David,
Tower of ivory,
House of gold,
Ark of the Covenant,
Gate of heaven,

Morning star,
Health of the sick,
Refuge of sinners,
Comforter of the afflicted,
Help of Christians,
Queen of angels,
Queen of patriarchs,
Queen of prophets,
Queen of apostles,
Queen of martyrs,
Queen of confessors,
Queen of virgins,
Queen of all saints,
Queen conceived without original sin,
Queen assumed into heaven,
Queen of the most holy rosary,
Queen of families,
Queen of peace,
Lamb of God, who take away the sins of the world,
spare us, O Lord.
Lamb of God, who take away the sins of the world,
graciously hear us, O Lord.
Lamb of God, who take away the sins of the world,
have mercy on us.
Pray for us, O holy Mother of God,
that we may be made worthy of the promises of
Christ.

Let us pray: Grant, we beseech You, O Lord God, that we Your servants may enjoy perpetual health of mind and body and, by the glorious intercession of the blessed Mary, ever virgin, be delivered from present sorrow, and obtain eternal joy. Through Christ our Lord. Amen.

We fly to your patronage, O holy Mother of God. Despise not our petitions in our necessities, but deliver us always from all dangers, O glorious and blessed Virgin. Amen.

8. **Prayer to St. Joseph.** St. Joseph, guardian of Jesus and chaste spouse of Mary, you passed your life in perfect fulfillment of duty. You supported the Holy Family of Nazareth with the work of your hands. Kindly protect those who trustingly turn to you. You know their aspirations, their hardships, their hopes; and they turn to you because they know you will understand and protect them. You too have known trial, labor, and weariness. But, even amid the worries of material life, your soul was filled with deep peace and sang out in true joy through intimacy with the Son of God entrusted to you, and with Mary, His tender Mother. Amen.

— (Pope John XXIII)

9. **Litany of the Sacred Heart, promises of the Sacred Heart.**
Lord, have mercy on us.
Christ, have mercy on us.
Lord, have mercy on us. Christ, hear us.
Christ, graciously hear us.
God the Father of heaven,
have mercy on us (repeat after each invocation).
God the Son, Redeemer of the world,
God the Holy Spirit,
Holy Trinity, one God,
Heart of Jesus, Son of the eternal Father,
Heart of Jesus, formed by the Holy Spirit in the womb of the Virgin Mother,
Heart of Jesus, substantially united to the Word of God,
Heart of Jesus, of infinite majesty,

Heart of Jesus, sacred temple of God,
Heart of Jesus, tabernacle of the Most High,
Heart of Jesus, house of God and gate of heaven,
Heart of Jesus, burning furnace of charity,
Heart of Jesus, abode of justice and love,
Heart of Jesus, full of goodness and love,
Heart of Jesus, abyss of all virtues,
Heart of Jesus, most worthy of all praise,
Heart of Jesus, king and center of all hearts,
Heart of Jesus, in whom are all the treasures of
   wisdom and knowledge,
Heart of Jesus, in whom dwells the fullness of
   divinity,
Heart of Jesus, in whom the Father is well pleased,
Heart of Jesus, of whose fullness we have all
   received,
Heart of Jesus, desire of the everlasting hills,
Heart of Jesus, patient and most merciful,
Heart of Jesus, enriching all who invoke You,
Heart of Jesus, fountain of life and holiness,
Heart of Jesus, propitiation for our sins,
Heart of Jesus, loaded down with opprobrium,
Heart of Jesus, bruised for our offenses,
Heart of Jesus, obedient even to death,
Heart of Jesus, pierced with a lance,
Heart of Jesus, source of all consolation,
Heart of Jesus, our life and reconciliation,
Heart of Jesus, victim of sin,
Heart of Jesus, salvation of those who hope in You,
Heart of Jesus, hope of those who die in You,
Heart of Jesus, delight of all the saints,
Lamb of God, Who take away the sins of the world,
   spare us, O Lord.
Lamb of God, Who take away the sins of the world,

graciously hear us, O Lord.
Lamb of God, Who take away the sins of the world,
have mercy on us.
Jesus, meek and humble of heart,
make our hearts like unto Yours.

Let us pray: O almighty and eternal God, look upon the Heart of Your dearly beloved Son and upon the praise and satisfaction He offers You in behalf of sinners and, being appeased, grant pardon to those who seek Your mercy, in the name of the same Jesus Christ, Your Son, Who lives and reigns with You, in the unity of the Holy Spirit, world without end. Amen.

Promises of Our Lord to those devoted to His Sacred Heart (these should be read by the prayer leader):

(1) I will give them all the graces necessary in their state of life.
(2) I will establish peace in their homes.
(3) I will comfort them in all their afflictions.
(4) I will be their refuge during life and above all in death.
(5) I will bestow a large blessing on all their undertakings.
(6) Sinners shall find in My Heart the source and the infinite ocean of mercy.
(7) Tepid souls shall grow fervent.
(8) Fervent souls shall quickly mount to high perfection.
(9) I will bless every place where a picture of My Heart shall be set up and honored.
(10) I will give to priests the gift of touching the most hardened hearts.
(11) Those who promote this devotion shall have their names written in My Heart, never to be blotted out.

(12) I promise you in the excessive mercy of My Heart that My all-powerful love will grant to all those who communicate on the first Friday in nine consecutive months the grace of final penitence; they shall not die in My disgrace nor without receiving their sacraments; My divine Heart shall be their safe refuge in this last moment.

10. **Prayer for Priests.** "Lord Jesus, Chief Shepherd of the Flock, we pray that in the great love and mercy of Your Sacred Heart You attend to all the needs of Your priest-shepherds throughout the world. We ask that You draw back to Your Heart all those priests who have seriously strayed from Your path, that You rekindle the desire for holiness in the hearts of those priests who have become lukewarm, and that You continue to give Your fervent priests the desire for the highest holiness. United with Your Heart and Mary's Heart, we ask that You take this petition to Your heavenly Father in the unity of the Holy Spirit. Amen."

11. **Prayer for all members of the Shepherds of Christ Associates.** "Dear Jesus, we ask Your special blessings on all members of Shepherds of Christ Associates. Continue to enlighten them regarding the very special privilege and responsibility you have given them as members of Your movement, Shepherds of Christ Associates. Draw them ever closer to Your Heart and to Your Mother's Heart. Allow them to more and more realize the great and special love of Your Hearts for each of them as unique individuals. Give them the grace to respond to Your love and Mary's love with an increased love of their own. As they dwell in Your Heart and Mary's Heart, abundantly care for all their needs and those of their loved ones. We make our

prayer through You to the Father, in the Holy Spirit, with Mary our Mother at our side. Amen."

12. **Prayer for the spiritual and financial success of the priestly newsletter.** "Father, we ask Your special blessings upon the priestly newsletter, Shepherds of Christ. We ask that You open the priest-readers to the graces You wish to give them through this chosen instrument of Your Son. We also ask that You provide for the financial needs of the newsletter and the Shepherds of Christ Associates. We make our prayer through Jesus, in the Holy Spirit, with Mary at our side. Amen."

13. **Prayer for all members of the human family.** "Heavenly Father, we ask Your blessings on all Your children the world over. Attend to all their needs. We ask Your special assistance for all those marginalized people, all those who are so neglected and forgotten. United with our Mother Mary, we make this petition to You through Jesus and in the Holy Spirit. Amen."

14. **Prayer to St. Michael and our Guardian Angels:** "St. Michael the Archangel, defend us in battle. Be our safeguard against the wickedness and snares of the devil. May God rebuke him, we humbly pray, and do thou, O prince of the heavenly hosts, by the power of God, cast into hell Satan and all the other evil spirits who prowl about the world seeking the ruin of souls. Amen."
"Angel of God, my guardian dear, to whom God's love commits me here, ever this day be at my side, to light and guard, to rule and guide. Amen."

15. **Pause for silent, personal prayer.** This should last at least five minutes.

16. **Act of consecration to the Sacred Heart of Jesus and the Immaculate Heart of Mary.**

"Lord Jesus, Chief Shepherd of the flock, I consecrate myself to Your most Sacred Heart. From Your pierced Heart the Church was born, the Church You have called me, as a member of Shepherds of Christ Associates, to serve in a most special way. You reveal Your Heart as a symbol of Your love in all its aspects, including Your most special love for me, whom You have chosen as Your companion in this most important work. Help me to always love You in return. Help me to give myself entirely to You. Help me always to pour out my life in love of God and neighbor! Heart of Jesus, I place my trust in You!

"Dear Blessed Virgin Mary, I consecrate myself to your maternal and Immaculate Heart, this Heart which is symbol of your life of love. You are the Mother of my Savior. You are also my Mother. You love me with a most special love as a member of Shepherds of Christ Associates, a movement created by your Son as a powerful instrument for the renewal of the Church and the world. In a return of love, I give myself entirely to your motherly love and protection. You followed Jesus perfectly. You are His first and perfect disciple. Teach me to imitate you in the putting on of Christ. Be my motherly intercessor so that, through your Immaculate Heart, I may be guided to an ever closer union with the pierced Heart of Jesus, Chief Shepherd of the flock."

17. **Daily Prayers.** All members should say the Holy Spirit prayer daily and make the act of consecration daily. They should also pray the rosary each day. They are encouraged to use the other above prayers as time allows.

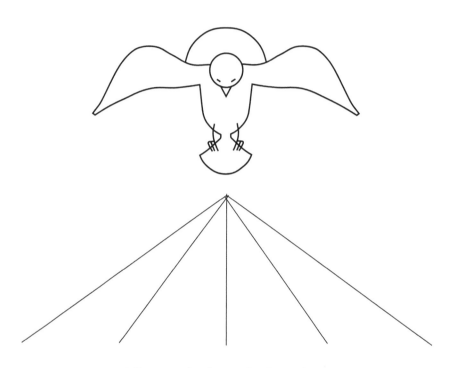

HOLY SPIRIT NOVENA

**The Holy Spirit Novnea prayers are
also available in
Spanish, French, and Portuguese.**

Shepherds of Christ Publications
China, Indiana

This book is published by Shepherds of Christ Publications, a subsidiary of Shepherds of Christ Ministries, a tax exempt religious public charitable association organized to foster devotion to the Two Hearts, the Sacred Heart of Jesus and the Immaculate Heart of Mary.

For additional copies, contact us:

Shepherds of Christ Ministries
P.O. Box 627
China, Indiana 47250 USA

(toll free number) 1-888-211-3041
(phone) 1-812-273-8405
(fax) 1-812-273-3182
http://www.SofC.org

Nihil Obstat:
Rev. Daniel J. Mahan, S.T.L.
Censor Librorum
Archdiocese of Indianapolis

Imprimatur:
Archbishop Daniel M. Buechlein, O.S.B.
Archbishop of Indianapolis
Archdiocese of Indianapolis

First Printing: March, 1999
Second Printing: April, 2000

DAILY NOVENA PRAYERS

Opening Prayer

In the name of the Father and of the Son and of the Holy Spirit. Amen.

Dear Father, we come to You in the name of Jesus, in union with Him in the Holy Sacrifice of the Mass, in the Holy Spirit. We come to You united to the Child Jesus of Good Health and the Infant of Prague. We come to You in the perfect, sinless heart of Our Mother Mary, asking her powerful intercession, uniting ourselves to her holy tears. We come to You united to all the angels and saints, and the souls in purgatory.

Prayer for Holy Spirit

We pray for an outpouring of the Holy Spirit on us, to be baptized by the Holy Spirit, that He will descend mightily on us as He did on the Apostles at Pentecost. That the Holy Spirit will transform us from fear to fearlessness and that He will give us courage to do all the Father is asking of us to help bring about the Reign of the Sacred Heart and the triumph of Mary's Immaculate Heart. We pray for the Holy Spirit to descend mightily on the Jesuits and the Poor Clares on the Shepherds of Christ leaders and members and on the whole Body of Christ and the world.

Protection by the Blood of Jesus

We pray that the Blood of Jesus will be spread on us, everyone in our families, and the Shepherds of Christ Movement, that we will be able to move steadfastly ahead and be protected from the evil one.

Healing

We pray for healing in body, mind, and soul and generational healing in ourselves, in all members in our families, and in all members of the Shepherds of Christ Movement, the Jesuit Community, the Poor Clares, the Body of Christ, and the world.

Prayer for Strength and Light

We adore You, oh Holy Spirit. Give us strength, give us light, console us. We give ourselves entirely to You. Oh Spirit of light and grace, we want to only do the will of the Father. Enlighten us that we may live always in the Father's will.

Eternal Spirit fill us with Your Divine Wisdom that we may comprehend more fully insight into Your Divine Mysteries.

Give us lights, Oh Holy Spirit that we may know God. Work within the heart, the spiritual womb of the Virgin Mary, to form us more and more into the image of Jesus.

Prayer to Be One with God, Father, Son and Holy Spirit

We long for You, Oh Spirit of Light, we long to know God, we want to be one with Him, our Divine God. We want to be one with the Father, know Him as a Person most intimately. We want to know the beloved One, the Sacred Heart of Jesus, and live and dwell in Him at all times, every moment of our lives. We want to be one with You, Oh Spirit of Light, that You move in us in our every breath.

Prayer to Be One in Jesus

Let us experience life in the Sacred Heart of Jesus, so we can say as Saint Paul, "I have been crucified with Christ and yet I am alive; yet it is no longer I, but Christ living in me...." Let us live, united to the Mass, all through the day being one in Him. Let us be able to love and know in this elevated state of oneness with our God. We long for Thee, oh beauteous God, we love You, we love You, we love You. We praise You, worship You, honor You, adore You, and thank You, our beloved God, Father, Son, and Holy Spirit.

Prayer to Dwell in the Hearts of Jesus and Mary

We seek to be one in God, to live and dwell in the Hearts of Jesus and Mary, our little heaven on earth, to experience life in the all perfect, pure, sinless heart of our Mother. We want the Holy Spirit to move in us and to be united to Jesus as the Bridegroom of our souls and be a most perfect sacrifice offered to the Father at every moment as we unite in the Holy Sacrifice of the Mass around the world to help in the salvation of souls.

Prayer for the Holy Spirit and His Gifts

Come Holy Spirit, come, come into our hearts, inflame all people with the fire of Your love.

Leader: Send forth Your Spirit and all will be reborn.

All: And You will renew the face of the earth.

We pray for the seven gifts of the Holy Spirit, we ask for perfection in our souls to make us holy, holy souls likened to God.

Dear Holy Spirit, we give ourselves to You soul and body. We ask You to give us the Spirit of Wisdom, Understanding, Counsel, Fortitude, Knowledge, Piety, and Fear of the Lord.

Prayer for the Word Alive in Our Hearts

We know, dear Holy Spirit, the Word in His human nature was brought forth within the womb of the woman. We pray that His word will be brought forth in our hearts as He lives and dwells in us. We want the incarnation to go on in our lives. Dear Holy Spirit, work in us.

Little Prayers to the Holy Spirit

Dear Holy Spirit, help us not to be ignorant or indifferent or weak, help us to be strong with the love of God.

Dear Holy Spirit, please pray for our needs for us.

Dear Holy Spirit, help us to respect God and to avoid sin. Help us to live in the Father's will.

Dear Holy Spirit, help us to keep Your commandments and to respect authority. Help us to love all things as You will us to love them. Help us to want to pray and always serve God with the greatest love. Help us to know the truth. Help us to have the gift of faith, hope, and love. Help us to know what is right and what is wrong.

A Prayer for Intimacy with the Lamb, the Bridegroom of the Soul

Oh Lamb of God, Who take away the sins of the world, come and act on my soul most intimately. I surrender myself, as I ask for the grace to let go, to just be as I exist in You and You act most intimately on my soul. You are the Initiator. I am the soul waiting Your favors as You act in me. I love You. I adore You. I worship You. Come and possess my soul with Your Divine Grace, as I experience You most intimately.

FIRST WEEK
MEDITATIONS NINE DAYS

1. Romans 8:14-17
All who are guided by the Spirit of God are sons of God; for what you received was not the spirit of slavery to bring you back into fear; you received the Spirit of adoption, enabling us to cry out, 'Abba, Father!' The Spirit himself joins with our spirit to bear witness that we are children of God. And if we are children, then we are heirs, heirs of God and joint-heirs with Christ, provided that we share his suffering, so as to share his glory.

2. Romans 8:5-9
Those who are living by their natural inclinations have their minds on the things human nature desires; those who live in the Spirit have their minds on spiritual things. And human nature has nothing to look forward to but death, while the Spirit looks forward to life and peace, because the outlook of disordered human nature is opposed to God, since it does not submit to God's Law, and indeed it cannot, and those who live by their natural inclinations can never be pleasing to God. You, however, live not by your natural inclinations, but by the Spirit, since the Spirit of God has made a home in you. Indeed, anyone who does not have the Spirit of Christ does not belong to him.

3. 1 John 4:12-16
No one has ever seen God, but as long as we love one another God remains in us and his love comes to its perfection in us. This is the proof that we remain in him and he in us, that he has given us a share in his Spirit. We ourselves have seen and testify that the Father sent his Son as Saviour of the world. Anyone who acknowledges that Jesus is the Son of God, God remains in him and he in God. We have recognised for

ourselves, and put our faith in, the love God has for us.
God is love, and whoever remains in love remains in
God and God in him.

4. 1 John 4:17-21
Love comes to its perfection in us when we can face
the Day of Judgement fearlessly, because even in this
world we have become as he is. In love there is no room
for fear, but perfect love drives out fear, because fear
implies punishment and no one who is afraid has come
to perfection in love. Let us love, then, because he first
loved us. Anyone who says 'I love God' and hates his
brother, is a liar, since whoever does not love the
brother whom he can see cannot love God whom he
has not seen. Indeed this is the commandment we have
received from him, that whoever loves God, must also
love his brother.

5. 1 John 4:7-11
My dear friends, let us love one another, since love
is from God and everyone who loves is a child of God
and knows God. Whoever fails to love does not know
God, because God is love. This is the revelation of
God's love for us, that God sent his only Son into the
world that we might have life through him. Love
consists in this: it is not we who loved God, but God
loved us and sent his Son to expiate our sins. My dear
friends, if God loved us so much, we too should love
one another.

6. Acts of the Apostles 1:1-5
In my earlier work, Theophilus, I dealt with
everything Jesus had done and taught from the
beginning until the day he gave his instructions to the
apostles he had chosen through the Holy Spirit, and
was taken up to heaven. He had shown himself alive
to them after his Passion by many demonstrations:
for forty days he had continued to appear to them and
tell them about the kingdom of God. While at table
with them, he had told them not to leave Jerusalem,

but to wait there for what the Father had promised. 'It is', he had said, 'what you have heard me speak about: John baptised with water but, not many days from now, you are going to be baptised with the Holy Spirit.'

7. Acts of the Apostles 1:6-9

Now having met together, they asked him, 'Lord, has the time come for you to restore the kingdom to Israel?' He replied, 'It is not for you to know times or dates that the Father has decided by his own authority, but you will receive the power of the Holy Spirit which will come on you, and then you will be my witnesses not only in Jerusalem but throughout Judaea and Samaria, and indeed to earth's remotest end.'

As he said this he was lifted up while they looked on, and a cloud took him from their sight.

8. Acts of the Apostles 1:12-14

So from the Mount of Olives, as it is called, they went back to Jerusalem, a short distance away, no more than a Sabbath walk; and when they reached the city they went to the upper room where they were staying; there were Peter and John, James and Andrew, Philip and Thomas, Bartholomew and Matthew, James son of Alphaeus and Simon the Zealot, and Jude son of James. With one heart all these joined constantly in prayer, together with some women, including Mary the mother of Jesus, and with his brothers.

9. Acts of the Apostles 2:1-4

When Pentecost day came round, they had all met together, when suddenly there came from heaven a sound as of a violent wind which filled the entire house in which they were sitting; and there appeared to them tongues as of fire; these separated and came to rest on the head of each of them. They were all filled with the Holy Spirit and began to speak different languages as the Spirit gave them power to express themselves.

SECOND WEEK
MEDITATIONS NINE DAYS

1. **John 14:21-31**
   Whoever holds to my commandments and keeps them is the one who loves me; and whoever loves me will be loved by my Father, and I shall love him and reveal myself to him.'

   Judas—not Judas Iscariot—said to him, 'Lord, what has happened, that you intend to show yourself to us and not to the world?' Jesus replied:

   'Anyone who loves me will keep my word, and my Father will love him, and we shall come to him and make a home in him. Anyone who does not love me does not keep my words. And the word that you hear is not my own: it is the word of the Father who sent me. I have said these things to you while still with you; but the Paraclete, the Holy Spirit, whom the Father will send in my name, will teach you everything and remind you of all I have said to you. Peace I bequeath to you, my own peace I give you, a peace which the world cannot give, this is my gift to you. Do not let your hearts be troubled or afraid. You heard me say: I am going away and shall return. If you loved me you would be glad that I am going to the Father, for the Father is greater than I. I have told you this now, before it happens, so that when it does happen you may believe.

   'I shall not talk to you much longer, because the prince of this world is on his way. He has no power over me, but the world must recognise that I love the Father and that I act just as the Father commanded. Come now, let us go.

2. **John 17:11-26**
   I am no longer in the world, but they are in the world, and I am coming to you. Holy Father, keep those you have given me true to your name, so that

they may be one like us. While I was with them, I kept those you had given me true to your name. I have watched over them and not one is lost except one who was destined to be lost, and this was to fulfil the scriptures. But now I am coming to you and I say these things in the world to share my joy with them to the full. I passed your word on to them, and the world hated them, because they belong to the world no more than I belong to the world. I am not asking you to remove them from the world, but to protect them from the Evil One. They do not belong to the world any more than I belong to the world. Consecrate them in the truth; your word is truth. As you sent me into the world, I have sent them into the world, and for their sake I consecrate myself so that they too may be consecrated in truth. I pray not only for these but also for those who through their teaching will come to believe in me. May they all be one, just as, Father, you are in me and I am in you, so that they also may be in us, so that the world may believe it was you who sent me. I have given them the glory you gave to me, that they may be one as we are one. With me in them and you in me, may they be so perfected in unity that the world will recognise that it was you who sent me and that you have loved them as you have loved me.

Father, I want those you have given me to be with me where I am, so that they may always see my glory which you have given me because you loved me before the foundation of the world. Father, Upright One, the world has not known you, but I have known you, and these have known that you have sent me. I have made your name known to them and will continue to make it known, so that the love with which you loved me may be in them, and so that I may be in them.

3. 1 Corinthians 15:20-28

In fact, however, Christ has been raised from the dead, as the first-fruits of all who have fallen asleep. As it was by one man that death came, so through one man has come the resurrection of the dead. Just as all die in Adam, so in Christ all will be brought to life; but all of them in their proper order: Christ the first-fruits, and next, at his coming, those who belong to him. After that will come the end, when he will hand over the kingdom to God the Father, having abolished every principality, every ruling force and power. For he is to be king until he has made his enemies his footstool, and the last of the enemies to be done away with is death, for he has put all things under his feet. But when it is said everything is subjected, this obviously cannot include the One who subjected everything to him. When everything has been subjected to him, then the Son himself will be subjected to the One who has subjected everything to him, so that God may be all in all.

4. Revelation 3:1-3,12,16-19

'Write to the angel of the church in Sardis and say, "Here is the message of the one who holds the seven spirits of God and the seven stars: I know about your behaviour: how you are reputed to be alive and yet are dead. Wake up; put some resolve into what little vigour you have left: it is dying fast. So far I have failed to notice anything in your behaviour that my God could possibly call perfect; remember how you first heard the message. Hold on to that. Repent! If you do not wake up, I shall come to you like a thief, and you will have no idea at what hour I shall come upon you.

Anyone who proves victorious I will make into a pillar in the sanctuary of my God, and it will stay there for ever; I will inscribe on it the name of my God and the name of the city of my God, the new Jerusalem which is coming down from my God in heaven, and my own new name as well.

'...but since you are neither hot nor cold, but only lukewarm, I will spit you out of my mouth. You say to yourself: I am rich, I have made a fortune and have everything I want, never realising that you are wretchedly and pitiably poor, and blind and naked too. I warn you, buy from me the gold that has been tested in the fire to make you truly rich, and white robes to clothe you and hide your shameful nakedness, and ointment to put on your eyes to enable you to see. I reprove and train those whom I love: so repent in real earnest.'

5. Revelation 5:9-14

They sang a new hymn: You are worthy to take the scroll and to break its seals, because you were sacrificed, and with your blood you bought people for God of every race, language, people and nation and made them a line of kings and priests for God, to rule the world.

In my vision, I heard the sound of an immense number of angels gathered round the throne and the living creatures and the elders; there were ten thousand times ten thousand of them and thousands upon thousands, loudly chanting:

Worthy is the Lamb that was sacrificed to receive power, riches, wisdom, strength, honour, glory and blessing. Then I heard all the living things in creation—everything that lives in heaven, and on earth, and under the earth, and in the sea, crying:

To the One seated on the throne and to the Lamb, be all praise, honour, glory and power, for ever and ever.

And the four living creatures said, 'Amen'; and the elders prostrated themselves to worship.

6. Revelation 7:14-17

I answered him, 'You can tell me, sir.' Then he said, 'These are the people who have been through the great trial; they have washed their robes white again in the blood of the Lamb. That is why they are standing in front of God's throne and serving him day and night in his sanctuary; and the One who sits on the throne will spread his tent over them. They will never hunger or thirst again; sun and scorching wind will never plague them, because the Lamb who is at the heart of the throne will be their shepherd and will guide them to springs of living water; and God will wipe away all tears from their eyes.'

7. Revelation 12:1-8

Now a great sign appeared in heaven: a woman, robed with the sun, standing on the moon, and on her head a crown of twelve stars. She was pregnant, and in labour, crying aloud in the pangs of childbirth. Then a second sign appeared in the sky: there was a huge red dragon with seven heads and ten horns, and each of the seven heads crowned with a coronet. Its tail swept a third of the stars from the sky and hurled them to the ground, and the dragon stopped in front of the woman as she was at the point of giving birth, so that it could eat the child as soon as it was born. The woman was delivered of a boy, the son who was to rule all the nations with an iron sceptre, and the child was taken straight up to God and to his throne, while the woman escaped into the desert, where God had prepared a place for her to be looked after for twelve hundred and sixty days.

And now war broke out in heaven, when Michael with his angels attacked the dragon. The dragon fought back with his angels, but they were defeated and driven out of heaven.

8. Revelation 14:1-7

Next in my vision I saw Mount Zion, and standing on it the Lamb who had with him a hundred and forty-four thousand people, all with his name and his Father's name written on their foreheads. I heard a sound coming out of heaven like the sound of the ocean or the roar of thunder; it was like the sound of harpists playing their harps. There before the throne they were singing a new hymn in the presence of the four living creatures and the elders, a hymn that could be learnt only by the hundred and forty-four thousand who had been redeemed from the world. These are the sons who have kept their virginity and not been defiled with women; they follow the Lamb wherever he goes; they, out of all people, have been redeemed to be the first-fruits for God and for the Lamb. No lie was found in their mouths and no fault can be found in them.

Then I saw another angel, flying high overhead, sent to announce the gospel of eternity to all who live on the earth, every nation, race, language and tribe. He was calling, 'Fear God and glorify him, because the time has come for him to sit in judgement; worship the maker of heaven and earth and sea and the springs of water.'

Revelation 19: 7-8

let us be glad and joyful and give glory to God, because this is the time for the marriage of the Lamb. His bride is ready, and she has been able to dress herself in dazzling white linen, because her linen is made of the good deeds of the saints.'

9. Revelation 21:1-10

Then I saw a new heaven and a new earth; the first heaven and the first earth had disappeared now, and there was no longer any sea. I saw the holy city, the new Jerusalem, coming down out of heaven from God, prepared as a bride dressed for her husband. Then I heard a loud voice call from the throne, 'Look, here God lives among human beings. He will make his home among them; they will be his people, and he will be their God, God-with-them. He will wipe away all tears from their eyes; there will be no more death, and no more mourning or sadness or pain. The world of the past has gone.'

Then the One sitting on the throne spoke. 'Look, I am making the whole of creation new. Write this, "What I am saying is trustworthy and will come true." ' Then he said to me, 'It has already happened. I am the Alpha and the Omega, the Beginning and the End. I will give water from the well of life free to anybody who is thirsty; anyone who proves victorious will inherit these things; and I will be his God and he will be my son. But the legacy for cowards, for those who break their word, or worship obscenities, for murderers and the sexually immoral, and for sorcerers, worshippers of false gods or any other sort of liars, is the second death in the burning lake of sulphur.'

One of the seven angels that had the seven bowls full of the seven final plagues came to speak to me and said, 'Come here and I will show you the bride that the Lamb has married.' In the spirit, he carried me to the top of a very high mountain, and showed me Jerusalem, the holy city, coming down out of heaven from God.

Revelation 22:20

The one who attests these things says: I am indeed coming soon.

Amen; come, Lord Jesus.

Scriptural quotations are taken from
The New Jerusalem Bible, Doubleday & Co.
Imprimatur granted by Cardinal Hume.

A Priest Is a Gift from God

by Rita Ring

REFRAIN

C   F   C   Am   C

A priest is a gift from God. A priest is a gift from God.

F   C   F   G

This is My Bod - y, This is My Blood, A

VERSES 1, 3

C   F   C   C   F   G

priest is a gift from God.
1. Come to Me, My chil - dren,
3. Come to Me, chil-dren of God,

C   F   G   C   F   G

I want to pos-sess your soul, I love you so ten - der - ly,
I want to pos-sess your soul, I give My - self to___ you

C   F   G   C   F   C

I want you to love Me too, A priest is a gift from God.
in the Ho - ly Eu - cha-rist, A priest is a gift from God.

F   G   C   F   C

I tell you My chil - dren, a priest is a gift from God. To -
I tell you My chil - dren, a priest is a gift from God. To -

F   G   C   F   G

day is the day the Lord has made, Wake, My chil-dren from your sleep,
day is the day the Lord has made, Wake, My chil-dren from your sleep,

A Song from Jesus

by Rita Ring

REFRAIN

F   Am

I come to you with great - est love, I

Dm   Am   B♭

am your lov - ing Sav - ior. I am your God, I

F   B♭   F

died for you, I come to you this day.

VERSES

F   Am

1. You are My pre - cious lit - tle one, I
2. Reach out to Me and do not fear, I

Dm   Am   B♭

love you oh so dear - ly. Come close to Me, My
want to be so close to you. You are My child, My

F   B♭   F   D.C.

lit - tle one, I loved you to My death.
pre - cious one, I love you ten - der - ly.

I Love You Jesus

by Rita Ring

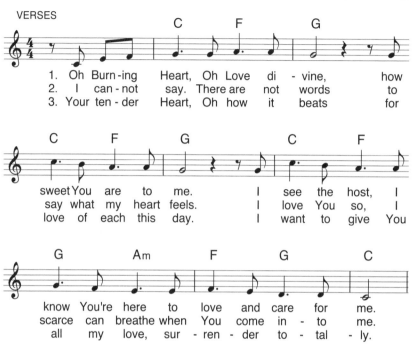

VERSES

1. Oh Burn-ing Heart, Oh Love di - vine, how
2. I can - not say. There are not words how to
3. Your ten - der Heart, Oh how it beats for

sweet You are to me. I see the host, I
say what my heart feels. I love You so, I
love of each this day. I want to give You

know You're here to love and care for me.
scarce can breathe when You come in - to me.
all my love, sur - ren - der to - tal - ly.

REFRAIN

I know Your love a lit - tle now, so

dear You are to me. Come give me life, a

bun - dant life, I thirst to be with Thee.

The Rosary Song

by Rita Ring

REFRAIN

Oh the ro-sa-ry, __ the ro-sa-ry __ is the
love of their two hearts, Oh the ro-sa-ry, __ the
ro-sa-ry __ is the love of their two hearts.

VERSES 1-4

1. A-ve Ma - ri - a, A-ve Ma - ri - a. Oh the
2. Je-sus we love You, Ma-ry we love__ you. Oh the
3. This is her peace plan, Chil-dren must pray__ it. Oh the
4. We turn to Ma-ry, She is the Queen of Peace. Oh the

VERSE 5

No left hand

5. Oh Sa-cred Heart di - vine, Oh heart of Ma-ry pure,

A - ve Ma - ri - a, We love to pray it! Oh the

Prayer for Union with Jesus

Come to me, Lord, and possess my soul. Come into my heart and permeate my soul. Help me to sit in silence with You and let You work in my heart.

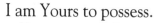

I am Yours to possess. I am Yours to use. I want to be selfless and only exist in You. Help me to spoon out all that is me and be an empty vessel ready to be filled by You. Help me to die to myself and live only for You. Use me as You will. Let me never draw my attention back to myself. I only want to operate as You do, dwelling within me.

I am Yours, Lord. I want to have my life in You. I want to do the will of the Father. Give me the strength to put aside the world and let You operate my very being. Help me to act as You desire. Strengthen me against the distractions of the devil to take me from Your work.

When I worry, I have taken my focus off of You and placed it on myself. Help me not to give in to the promptings of others to change what in my heart You are making very clear to me. I worship You, I adore You and I love You. Come and dwell in me now.

Shepherds of Christ
Prayer Cards and Books

Contact us to obtain
these for your parish,
friends, or loved ones.

Consecration to Mary

Dear Mary, my holy mother, I love you so much and I give you my heart. Help me to love God. Help me to love my neighbor as a child of God. Help me to love myself as a child of God.

Amen

2009 © SHEPHERDS OF CHRIST PUBLICATIONS

Consecration to Jesus

Dear Sacred Heart of Jesus, I love You so much and I give You my heart. Help me to love God. Help me to love my neighbor as a child of God. Help me to love myself as a child of God.

Amen

2009 © SHEPHERDS OF CHRIST PUBLICATIONS

Rita Robinson Ring and Fr. Joseph Robinson

Other great books published by
Shepherds of Christ Publications

(To order call or write us at address in front of book)

Shepherds of Christ Prayer Manual
The Shepherds of Christ has prayer chapters all over the world praying for the priests, the Church and the world. These prayers that Father Carter compiled in the summer of 1994 began this worldwide network of prayer. Currently the prayers are in eight languages with the Church's *Imprimatur*. We have prayed daily for the priests, the Church, and the world since 1994. Associates are called to join prayer Chapters and help us circulate the newsletter centered on spreading devotion to the Sacred Heart and Immaculate Heart and helping to renew the Church through greater holiness. Please form a Prayer Chapter & order a Prayer Manual. Item P1 - $0.50

Spirituality Handbook Fr. Edward Carter, S.J. did 3 synopsis of the spiritual life. *The Spirituality Handbook, the Priestly Newsletter 2000 Issue 3* and the *Tell My People* book. The way of spiritual life proposed to the members of Shepherds of Christ Associates is centered in consecration to the Hearts of Jesus and Mary. All aspects of the spiritual life discussed below should be viewed as means to help members develop their lives in consecration to Christ, the Sacred Heart, and to Mary, the Immaculate Heart. Item P2 - $3

Fr. Edward J. Carter S.J.

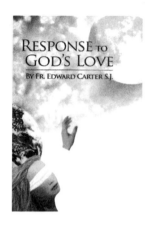

Response to God's Love by Fr. Edward J. Carter, S.J. In this book Fr. Carter speaks of God as the ultimate mystery. We can meditate on the interior life of the Trinity. Fr. Carter tells us about our uniqueness in the Father's Plan for us, how the individual Christian, the Church and the world are in the state of becoming. *Imprimatur.* Item BN4 -$10

Shepherds of Christ - Selected Writings on Spirituality for all People as Published in Shepherds of Christ Newsletter for Priests. Contains 12 issues of the newsletter from July/August 1994 to May/June 1996. Item BN1 - $15

Shepherds of Christ - Volume 2 by Fr. Edward J. Carter, S.J. Contains issues 13-29 of the Priestly newsletter (September / October 1996 - Issue 5, 1999) Item BN2 - $15

Fr. Edward J. Carter S.J.

Shepherds of Christ - Volume 3 by Fr. Edward J. Carter, S.J. Contains Priestly Newsletter Issues 1 through 4 of 2000 including Fr. Carter's tremendous *Overview of the Spiritual Life*
Item BN3 - $10

Rita Ring

Mass Book, by Rita Ring. Many of the entries in the Priestly Newsletter Volume II from a spiritual journal came from this book. These entries are to help people to be more deeply united to God in the Mass. This book is available in English and Spanish with the Church's *Imprimatur*.
Item B8 - $12

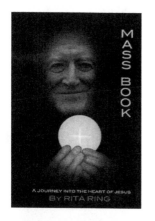

Parents and Children's Rosary Book, by Rita Ring. Short Meditations for both parents and children to be used when praying the rosary. These medi-tations will help all to know the lives of Jesus and Mary alive in their Hearts. Available in both English and Spanish with the Church's *Imprimatur*.
Item B7 - $10

Fr. Joe Robinson
(Rita Ring's Brother)

Guiding Light homily series - Steadfast to the Son - Cycle A — The sunflower is a great example of how we should be steadfastly guided by light. What a powerful thought that this exceptional plant is not stuck in one pose day in and day out, yet adaptable and magnetized to the sun. We feel the same about our Son. Our heads turns to face Christ as each day presents its challenges to find light. We join together like plants in a field and soak up the Son through the pulpit. We are a warm circle of strength using the wind of our breath to carry our priests' words, Christ's words, to new rich soil. Item C4 - $15

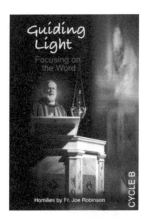

Guiding Light - Focusing on the Word - Cycle B — At times we may feel that our path to Christ is a bit "out of focus". Like the disciples in the Book of Mark, this ordinary life clouds our vision of Christ's Divinity. We may doubt the practicality or possibility of applying His teachings and example to our modern life. Cycle B's homilies are a "guiding light" to help us realize Jesus' Messianic greatness and His promise of better things to come. Item C2 - $15

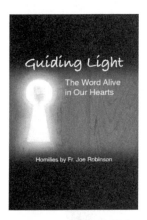

Guiding Light - The Word Alive in Our Hearts. - Cycle A (partial) — Homilies by the Reverend Joe Robinson given at St. Boniface Church in Cincinnati, Ohio. It is a tremendous honor Fr. Joe has allowed us to share these great gifts with you – for greater holiness and knowing more and more about God. Item C1 - $5

Fr. Joe Robinson

Guiding Light - Feed My Soul - Cycle C — In a world rapidly advancing and encouraging personal gain, we are faced with modern problems. There is a challenge to find time in our busy schedules for Sunday Mass or a family meal. We are able to research, shop, bank and even work without hearing one human voice. It is no wonder that we may often feel disconnected and famished at our week's end. In Fr. Joe's third book of homilies from Cycle C, we are reminded of the charity that Christ intended us to show each other. We have a calling to turn the other cheek and be the Good Samaritan to others. We are rewarded with the Father's kingdom and love when we are not worthy. We are not left alone or hungry. Item C3 - $15

Guiding Light - Reflect on the Word - Cycle B — The Word leaves an impression on our souls. In my thoughts and reflections are born a more tangible understanding of these eternal concepts presented in the Gospels and the readings. Anyone can read a sentence, but not anyone can absorb it's true meaning. Truth, in this day and age, is almost a matter of opinion or individual entitlement. We believe that Christ's truth is our Roman Catholic Church. We, as priests, champion it's teachings; we are ambassadors for the Pope and Christ to those faces looking at us. We are the light by which our congregation reads to reflect upon real truth and we do it hand in hand. Item C5 - $15

Featured Selections

Response in Christ by Fr. Carter

The book, *Response in Christ,* comes at a very opportune time. In a thoughtful blend of the traditional and the modern, Fr. Carter gives to the modern Christian a message that will sustain him.

The most promising aspect of the book is Fr. Carter's gift about the Spiritual life. The Christian life essentially consists in God's loving self-communication to us with our response to Him in love. God gives us a sharing in His life in baptism. This life is nourished by the Eucharist. Father Carter offers reflections on how to deepen one's relationship with God: Father, Son and Holy Spirit. Item BN5 -$10

Centered In Christ, Cycle C by Fr. Joseph Robinson

Total Commitment

In the gospel of St. Luke, Christ turns toward Jerusalem, making the choice of love through sacrifice. In the silence of our own hearts, we find a worthy call to action. What personal path will you chose as you center in Jesus Christ?

Fr. Joseph Robinson has dedicated his life to serving Christ and the Church from the Cincinnati Archdiocese in Ohio for over 40 years. He inspires his parishioners with the homilies found in these pages. They are not only practical, but also filled with light humor and a sense of hope, the hope of living out the Gospel despite today's challenges. May they be a guiding light for you as they have been for so many others.

Item BN6 -$10

Shepherds of Christ Ministries

(You may copy this page to order.)

Send Order To:
Shepherds of Christ Ministries
P.O. Box 627
China, Indiana 47250 USA

Order Form

	Qty	Total $
P1. Prayer Manuals ($0.50)	____	_____
P2. Spirituality Handbook ($3)	____	_____
BN4. Response to God's Love ($10)	____	_____
BN1. Shepherds of Christ - Volume 1 ($15)	____	_____
BN2. Shepherds of Christ - Volume 2 ($15)	____	_____
BN3. Shepherds of Christ - Volume 3 ($10)	____	_____
B8. Mass Book ($12)	____	_____
B7. Parents and Children's Rosary Book ($10)	____	_____
C4. Steadfast to the Son - Cycle A ($15)	____	_____
C2. Focusing on the Word - Cycle B ($15)	____	_____
C1. The Word Alive in Our Hearts ($5)	____	_____
C3. Feed My Soul - Cycle C ($15)	____	_____
C5. Reflect on the Word - Cycle B ($15)	____	_____
BN5. Response in Christ ($10)	____	_____
BN6. Centered in Christ ($10)	____	_____
Totals:	____	_____

Name: _____

Address: _____

City: _____ State: _____ Zip: _____

For More Information Call Toll free USA: 1-888-211-3041
or on the Internet: www.sofc.org

We pray for you from our Church in China,
24 hours a day before the exposed Eucharist.

We pray eight-day retreats for you every month.